A College Student

Dr. Bill Nesbitt's book broadens my understanding of Christianity by integrating Biblical concepts with scientific theories. He examines our universe in its relation to higher dimensions and uses analogies from real life experiences to illustrate his assumptions.

Brandon Minto
University of California, Davis

An International High School Youth Leader

Over the years I have worked with a wide variety of young people who would find this book very interesting and helpful in their faith journey. Christian teachers, Bible scholars and ministers will be fascinated by its challenging concepts. I especially see a strong market for this book among high school and college students.

Robert Mitchell
Past President, Young Life International

Professor of English

True art, it's said, is making the difficult appear easy. With stunning analogies, Dr. Bill Nesbitt has done just that — made difficult concepts comprehensible and inspiring.

Pat Wellington, Ph.D.
Professor of English
University of Miami (Retired)

High School Science Teachers

A mind opening and challenging look at past beliefs that lead to a new understanding of God's Kingdom. This is a story of faith and trust in God that will inspire readers whether they are laymen or scientists.

Robert and Myrlee Potosnak (joint statement)
Both are retired high school science teachers
Fairfield-Suisun Unified School District

Deep Space Microwave Research Engineer

This book presents a different and interesting viewpoint of higher dimensions, the nearness of heaven, and how God sees us. If God sees our lives from beginning to end, including the things we are going to do, it gives us considerable food for thought. Sending His Son to forgive our sins, past, present and future gives us much to thank Him for.

Norman Proebstel
Deep Space Microwave Research Engineer, (Ret.)
NASA, Goldstone Project

C-5 Pilot, United States Air Force

Science and theology have been at odds for quite awhile. Dr. Nesbitt's book will help erase the misconceptions these two disciplines have about each other. The basic theme of his assumptions is to point us all to Jesus Christ.

Willis Rice
Lieutenant Colonel,
United States Air Force (Retired)

A High School Student

This book has some cool ideas. Although I don't fully understand all the scientific concepts it stimulates my desire to learn more about how science confirms scripture. Knowing there are sound arguments for believing the Bible strengthens my faith in Christianity.

John Emerick
Dexter High School, (Dexter Michigan)

THE ILLUSION OF TIME

Seeing Scripture Through Science

By

William R. Nesbitt, M.D.

Black Forest Press
San Diego, California
March, 2002
First Edition

THE ILLUSION OF TIME

Seeing Scripture Through Science

By

William R. Nesbitt, M.D.

PUBLISHED IN THE UNITED STATES OF AMERICA
BY
BLACK FOREST PRESS
P.O. Box 6342
Chula Vista, CA 91909-6342

Dedication

This book is dedicated to my wife Bernice, who, in spite of her illness, contributed to its successful completion in many intangible ways.

"And we know that in all things God works for the good of those who love Him." **Romans 8: 28**

Cover Design by
Alan Skinner

Artistic Consultant
Eleanor Kessler

Printed in the United States of America
Library of Congress
Cataloging-in-Publication

ISBN: 1-58275-075-0

Acknowledgements

At the year 2000 Mount Hermon Christian Writer's Conference, David Kopp, Director of Product Development and Senior Editor for Multnomah Publishers, challenged me to write a book on the relationship of higher dimensions to theology. I had just received the conference "2000 Writer of the Year Award" and I was basking in the sunshine of my recent success in writing for leading Christian periodicals. I was not particularly interested in taking on such a Herculean task at my age (85 years old). Knowing the time it would take to write such a manuscript, find a publisher for such an esoteric subject, and get the book published was something I didn't look forward to, but David insisted it was something I had to do.

Now, it is with deep appreciation that I acknowledge David's important role in the inception and consummation of this project. The personal rewards of expanding my knowledge in the field of hyperdimensional theory as it relates to the Bible are incalculable.

✦　　✦　　✦　　✦　　✦

Without acquiring the writing skills I so desperately needed to write and publish a manuscript of this nature, my work would have been a dismal failure; so I must give credit to those who have shared their time and energy to teach me the craft of writing. Therefore, I would like to thank the following people for their part in forwarding my writing career.

Hal Hostetler, Editor for *Guideposts* magazine, whose help, patience and understanding launched me on my road to success by helping me get my first published article in *Guideposts*.

Debbie Hedstrom, whose brilliant course on "Writing for the Beginner" taught me the techniques of effectively transposing thoughts into print.

Holly Miller, Editor of *Saturday Evening Post*, for her guidance in my struggle to get the first chapter out of the doldrums of boredom into the realm of readability.

My niece, Dr. Pat Wellington, Professor of English, University of Miami, (Ret.) whose enthusiasm, wisdom and technical skill greatly assisted me with punctuation and grammar. Her editing, suggestions, patience and encouragement gave me hope that I could finish the project.

Leonard Meuer, a computer specialist, and close personal friend, provided valuable assistance in making my computer behave itself and do what I wanted it to do. Without his selfless oversight it would have taken me years to finish this book.

Another group of people without whose help I could never have accomplished this project are my family, my ancillary helpers, and the many friends who critiqued my manuscript, discussed my assumptions and offered valuable suggestions. I especially owe a debt of gratitude to my three children. My daughter, Dr. Barbara Emerick, a dentist with a large private dental practice and a Research Investigator at the University of Michigan, made the following comment about my manuscript, "Thoughtful and compelling; an original and thoughtful concept relating time and space to everyday life. It combines the latest theories of science with conservative theology." My eldest son Dr. William Nesbitt (III), a practicing physician and also a writer for Christian periodicals, states, "This book illustrates that science is catching up with theology, and not eroding scriptural credibility." My youngest son Dr. Tom Nesbitt, Associate Professor of Family Practice and Assistant Dean of the University of California Davis, School of Medicine says, "This book challenges some of our most basic beliefs about the nature of our existence, at the same time creating a fascinating new paradigm that incorporates both Christian theology and current scientific theory about time and space."

I include these comments not for the purpose of recording the plaudits of my children, but because they were my most severe critics during the composition of this work. Because they contested my reasoning at every turn I was forced to rethink and clarify many of my assumptions.

I want to thank Dr. Ken Dod, a life long friend, who read and reread my manuscript as it took shape and made many useful comments.

I also want to thank Elvia Robin, caregiver for my wife Bernice, who comes to our house five mornings a week to bathe, dress and give my wife hygienic care. She affirms my faith that angels are real people.

Roland Hortensius, a retired missionary and a skilled handy man, who has relieved me of the responsibility of maintaining a large country home.

Bob Wegener, a good friend and an inactive Catholic Priest, who enthusiastically supported most of my assumptions and contributed his Near Death Experience to my chapter on Redefining Death.

Bud Stevenson, a stockbroker and a professed skeptic, who spent hours with me debating the validity of my assumptions. He is an avid reader, and even though he would not admit to the logic of my assumptions, he would frequently bring me articles from secular sources supporting my contentions.

I thank, from the bottom of my heart, these wonderful friends, and the many others who patiently listened to my extraordinary assumptions and then made constructive comments.

Bill Nesbitt

Any interested reader desiring communication with the author, Dr. William Nesbitt, M.D., concerning this book (for the discussion of related topics of personal interest, or making beneficial and relevant comments, or asking subject matter questions or for submitting new religious and/or scientific contributions) may email, or write to the following addresses:

Email: billn@jps.net

Author's mailing address:
    P.O. Box 192 Fairfield, CA, 94533-0019

All reader comments are welcomed and appreciated. God bless each of you and thank you for your support and interest in my work.
Dr. William Nesbitt, M.D.

*Response to comments and suggestions will only be answered in exceptional cases.

Publisher Commentary: You, the reader, are in for a significant learning adventure. You will ask yourself the question if time IS an illusion? How will this theory (which is very reasonable and rational) impact modern religious thought? The opportunities and possibilities for developing and exploring advanced thinking, by entering into a new world full of probability yet still an enigma, is exciting and thought provoking. When you complete Dr. Nesbitt's book, you will most likely never view the world around you, as you have before.

Dahk Knox, Ph.D., Ed.D.
CEO/Publisher, Black Forest Press

About the Author

Dr. William Nesbitt is a retired physician and surgeon with the degrees of Bachelor of Science in Medicine and Doctor of Medicine from Duke University. During World War II he was commissioned a Medical Officer in the United States Navy. During the Normandy Invasion, he landed on Omaha Beach with the first medical support wave of the Navy's 7th Beach Battalion and later served as a Military Government Officer in the South Pacific. Following a brief change of status to the inactive reserve, he returned to active duty during the Korean War and still holds the rank of Lieutenant Commander (MC) USNR (Ret.)

For twenty years, he was in private general practice in California. Following this period of private practice, he was appointed to a full time faculty position at the University of California, Davis School of Medicine. Upon retiring from the University, he accepted an appointment as Chief of Disaster Medical Services for the California Department of Health Services, and served as Disaster Medical Coordinator for the State of California.

At the mandatory retirement age of seventy, he left employment with the State and accepted a position as Medical Director for Helgeson Scientific Services. In this capacity he conducted medical response training courses and disaster drills for nuclear accidents at nuclear power plants throughout the United States.

At age eighty-three, he took up freelance writing for Christian periodicals. His byline has appeared in a number of national and international religious magazines including *Guideposts, Focus On the Family, Moody Magazine, Decision, The Upper Room* and others.

Dr. Nesbitt was born in Baltimore, Maryland, March 12, 1914. Both his parents were ordained ministers. He was raised in a home with solid Biblical values that he has incorporated into his own life from early childhood. He was ordained an Elder in the Presbyterian Church at the age of twenty-four and has served in this capacity in several different Presbyterian congregations.

In the Navy, private practice and academia he served the Lord in various ways: He has served on the National Board of Directors of Young Life and he has been a board member and president of Refugees International. He has also been a conference speaker, a Bible class teacher, and a Christian counselor for most of his professional career.

His wife, Bernice a devout Christian, was a professional educator and school administrator before her early retirement due to a serious illness. Dr. and Mrs. Nesbitt have three adult children, all committed Christians: a daughter, who is a dentist, and two sons who are physicians.

Dr. Nesbitt and his wife live in Fairfield, California, and attend the Fairfield Presbyterian Church, where they both have served as Elders.

Bible translations used were *King James* and *New International* Version.

Contents

Figures

Foreword

In November 2001 I escaped from the toils of working life by spending a few days on the island of Maui. It was meant to be a time when I would allow myself to mentally vegetate. But that was not to be for I carried with me a draft of this book that Dr. William R. Nesbitt had asked me to review for comment...of any kind. As a friend, and admirer, of Dr. Nesbitt for nearly twenty years it seemed I would have the pleasure of peeking into the mind of a man I knew to be a devoted Christian physician. My expectations were to learn a little bit more of modern Christian thinking. That's all, nothing more. To my surprise I was to embark upon a journey that stretched my knowledge and understanding of science and the scriptures beyond anything I had ever read before.

We who live at the beginning of the 21st century are accustomed to the never ending arguments from two camps: the science-rationalists and the religious fundamentalists. Since the Age of Reason, or Enlightenment, it has seemed that those two camps were moving farther away from each other without any hope of reconciliation or accommodation. Between them sits a majority of people who walk the fence believing that both camps have some truths to their arguments, but neither knows the complete truth. From Galileo onward mankind has watched the many, extraordinary advancements in science that have come in direct conflict with religious authority or teaching. As we learn more about ourselves and our universe, each camp finds solace in the revelation of "new truths." For example, some would say the idea of a "big bang" has brought a scientific revelation that God "willed" the universe into existence at a single moment...as only God could do.

No matter who you are, no matter the intensity of your religious beliefs, no matter the breadth of your scientific education, Dr. Nesbitt will jar your comfort level with his challenging concepts. Among these are:

Heaven is not in the direction you think it is. It is not up in the sky. The Garden of Eden was not on this

Earth, and may still exist. Heaven is much closer than you think, maybe as close as one millimeter.

The question that must come to the reader's mind is, how can one ever scientifically walk through the scriptures, especially in those areas where its mysteries are accepted on faith. How can the cosmology of Genesis be reconciled with overwhelming evidence of the Earth's antiquity? And if those questions are not challenging, be prepared to deal with the concept that time and space are finite and that nothing moves and nothing changes.

It is through "hyperdimensional theory" that Dr. Nesbitt will take you through this new "looking glass" of the universe. More than that he will weave throughout his book glimpses into his own personal life, a life that ran the gamut of his near death in a childhood auto accident to facing death again, landing on the beaches of Normandy in the 1944 D-Day invasion of World War II. But through all of these concepts and adventures, he ultimately will challenge you to surrender your life to Jesus Christ.

William R. Rawlinson,
Colonel United States Air Force, (Ret.)
Fairfield, California
December 7, 2001

Colonel Rawlinson, following a tour of duty as Base Commander of Travis Air Force Base, California, was promoted to Chief of Staff, Headquarters, 22nd Air Force, Travis Air Force Base, California.

Following his retirement from the Air Force he was employed for nine years as cash Operations Manager for the Federal Reserve Bank of San Francisco.

For 21 years he has been Adjunct Instructor of Business and Management, Solano Community College, Fairfield, California.

For the past three years he has been President of California- Nevada North State Association of Gideons International.

ii

Preface

Read about a medical doctor's search for Biblical under-standing in the arcane world of modern science. By restructuring traditional concepts of time and space the authenticity of the scriptures take on new meaning. Salvation, the final judgment, a picture of heaven and hell, eternal life, the forgiveness of sins, miracles, creation, the occult, the nearness of God, answers to prayer, death, the resurrection of the dead, healing and many difficult Biblical passages in the Bible on these subjects can be better understood in the light of the latest scientific theories.

Dr. Nesbitt's studies have brought him to some astounding assumptions. Based on sound Biblical information and the latest scientific theories, he discovered that some traditional theological concepts might be better understood in the light of cutting edge scientific theories.

Some of the assumptions are:

1. Heaven is not in the direction you think it is. It's not up in the sky.
2. There's a model of creation that is more Biblical and more logical than the traditional ones.
3. The Garden of Eden was not on this earth, and may still exist.
4. Joshua's 'long day' was not a threat to the controlling forces of our solar system by altering centrifugal force and gravity that are responsible for maintaining the delicate and critical balance needed for the integrity of planetary relationships.
5. Adam and Eve had children before they sinned, and they are still living today.
6. Before Adam and Eve sinned death was not inevitable.
7. There is an answer to the question, "Who is Melchizedek?"
8. Physical heavenly beings have frequently visited the earth and they continue to do so.

9. Heaven is much closer than you think. Maybe as close as one millimeter.

10. Hyperdimensional theory provides a basis for a logical understanding of a Monotheistic Triune God.

11. Many of the miracles in the Bible can be explained by scientific theories that require power beyond the capabilities of man to generate.

12. Time and space are finite; nothing moves, nothing changes. Everything you've ever done, everything you've ever said, everything you've ever thought is still being said done and thought in the long body of your past: — unless you are a Christian.

13. Jesus said, "*Be ye therefore perfect even as your Father in heaven is perfect.*" **Matthew. 5:48**; but **1 John 2:4** says, "*He who says he is without sin is a liar and the truth is not in him.*" There is a simple answer to this paradox.

14. Every person who ever lived past, present and future has, or has had, the opportunity to hear the gospel of salvation. There is an answer as to how this could be.

15. Those who we believe have died are not actually physically dead.

16. Job said: "*And after my skin has been destroyed, yet in my flesh I will see God; I myself will see him with my own eyes—I, and not another.*" **Job 19:26,27** How can this be? Theoretical physics has the answer.

17. Heaven is a place of physical reality just as tangible as the reality we experience on earth.

18. Teleportation is mentioned in the Bible: "*When they came up out of the water*, **the Spirit of the Lord suddenly took Philip away, Philip, however, appeared at Azotus.**" *Acts 8: 39-40* There's a scientific theory that can explain this miraculous event.

19. We know there will be animals in heaven. There is a possibility they may be your pets, and the exciting part is there is scriptural precedent that they may be able to talk to you.

20. The Bible mentions *soul sleep* in a number of places, but it also says absent from the body, present with the Lord. There is a logical answer.

The above statements are based on conclusions derived from reputable scientific literature. It's not indisputable science and Dr. Nesbitt is not proposing new theological dogma. What he's trying to do is crack the shell of traditional thinking and open up vast new areas of information for exploration that will add substance to the defense of the Christian Faith.

Before acquiring this knowledge Dr. Nesbitt said that scientists and other academics intimidated him when he attempted to defend his Biblical beliefs. Now, using *their* secular theories he believes he can stand his ground when questioned about his Faith.

Introduction

"One thing I do know. I was blind but now I see!" **John 9:25**

Time is an illusion. Time is not what you think it is. Time can bend, it can stop and it can speed up. It's affected by gravity and there was a period in Biblical chronology when the passage of time did not accur.

Time and space can not be seperated from each other. Time–space is finite. It has a beginning and it has an end. The remarkable thing is that understanding the characteristics of time and space helps us to understand the scriptures.

Thousands of years ago the Bible made statements that are compatible with the theories of modern physics. Those statements in the Scriptures, made in the days of primitive scientific knowledge, have turned out to be amazingly accurate. Using stories and information from scientific sources, we will explore the correlation of modern thought about the world we live in and the world the Bible described so accurately long ago. God is just as precise in the structure and operation of His spiritual creation as He is in regard to His physical creation. Scientists are now proving themselves to be wrong about the things in the Bible they said were impossible. Jesus said, *"With man this is impossible, but with God all things are possible."* **Matthew 19:26** Now we can boldly express our belief in the Biblical record and defend it against ridicule by scientists.

Academicians have recently become excited about the mystical world of theoretical physics. The impossible has become feasible; the inconceivable has become understandable and the fictional has become historical. From the macrocosm to the microcosm, traditional concepts have given way to new ideas that stagger the imagination. Scientists are seriously investigating theories of higher dimensions, multiple universes and wormholes; ideas that until recently were relegated to science fiction.

Our minds reel when confronted with the complexity of the genome project, nano-technology, experiments altering the speed of light and the restructuring of our ideas of time and space. These theories impact the 'sacred cows' of traditional science and philosophy. They bring into question the theory of evolution, the curvature of space, the true characteristics of time and the absolute character and speed of light.

One would think that serious consideration of the esoteric subjects of science would be distract from the reality of our spiritual relationship with God, but paradoxically they support the integrity of the Bible. I would like you to join me as we try to resolve the paradox of compatability between the two seemingly disparate subjects of science and theology.

✦   ✦   ✦   ✦   ✦

I grasped the podium with sweaty hands; my knees were like jelly and my heart was racing. It was not the audience of doctors, military officers, government officials and others interested in our national defense that made me nervous. It was that one person who could demolish my presentation.

I was speaking at the annual meeting of TACDA (The American Civil Defense Association) in Huntsville, Alabama, October 1992. My topic was *Medical Implications of the Widespread Contamination of the Environment in Russia by Radioactive Materials.*

As Chief of Disaster Medical Services for the State of California, I had prepared a Medical Nuclear Incident Response Plan for use by the Governor's Office of Emergency Services. The threat of a radiation emergency in California ranged from a highway spill of radioactive material, or a nuclear power plant accident, to nuclear terrorism, or even the outright use of atomic weapons. I knew my material well, but my presentation preceded a talk by Dr. Edward Teller, father of the hydrogen bomb, consultant to presidents and world acclaimed physicist. He had recently returned from Russia, where he had evaluated firsthand the problem I was to discuss. I was way out of my comfort zone.

But where was he? I looked at the audience; Dr. Teller was not present. Breathing a sigh of relief, I launched into a vivid description of the magnitude of the problem Russia faced in trying to decontaminate vast areas of land and water polluted by nuclear waste.

My relief was short-lived. Scarcely had I uttered my first few sentences when the back door of the auditorium opened and Dr. Teller appeared. He reminded me of Father Time, tall, stooped and with a five-foot staff he uses for a cane, he came thumping down the isle and seated himself in the second row.

During my presentation, he sat with his head bowed and his eyes closed. I was hoping he was either asleep, or lost in thought about some esoteric problem in theoretical physics. Since he seemed to be paying no attention to what I was saying, I relaxed and finished my talk.

It's customary at these meetings to allow time for questions, so after I concluded my formal presentation I invited, with trepidation, questions from the floor. Dr. Teller's hand shot up.

"Yes, Dr. Teller, do you have a question?"

Surely my goose was cooked; the world's top authority on nuclear matters didn't need to ask a neophyte like me a question about a subject on which he was the ultimate authority. I grasped the podium more firmly and waited.

Dr. Teller remained seated and said, "I don't have a question, but I would like to make some comments about the talk we have just heard. Dr. Nesbitt has given an excellent introduction to Russia's problems with environmental contamination by nuclear materials, but he has only scratched the surface of their magnitude." He went on to say that from his personal observations, the world has no idea how bad the situation is. "It will take hundreds of years and trillions of dollars to clean up the contamination." There being no more comments, I left the platform greatly relieved.

Later, over refreshments, I asked Dr. Teller a question that has bothered me for many years. It was about an exhibit I saw at the Griffith Park Planetarium in Los Angeles. The exhibit raised questions about the relation of time and motion. The implication was that the appearance of motion by physical objects is an illusion.

"That's scientific gobbledygook," he said flatly.

Before I had the opportunity to ask why, others interrupted our conversation.

I'm telling this story because I feel similar trepidation as I write this book. I see scientists and theologians, entrenched in their conventional concepts, thumping down the aisle, seating themselves on the front row and waiting for me to make a foolish mistake so they can discredit what I'm about to say.

✦   ✦   ✦   ✦   ✦

My interest in the application of the theory of higher dimensions to theology began at the age of fifteen, following an accident in which I was seriously injured. Everyone, including me, thought I was going to die. I made an irrevocable commitment of my life to God and put my future in His hands.

For four years, I was unable to attend school. When I was able to resume my education, I went to a small private school where I took an accelerated program to make up some of the time I'd lost.

The small private junior college in Berkeley, California I attended required all students to take an orientation course. The course was not about orienting students to their school environment, but rather to the world, and all of life in general. For the first time, I heard about the fourth dimension. I was so fascinated by the subject that I looked for more information. In my search, I came across a book titled, *The Fourth Dimension and the Bible*, by **William Anthony Granville**, a mathematician, and the President of Gettysburg College. In the preface to this book he wrote, "The author's chief aim will be to point out the remarkable agreement which exists between numerous Bible passages and some of the concepts which follow quite naturally from the mathematical hypothesis of higher space."

Over the years, I've discussed the assumptions with anyone who would listen. The application of higher dimensions to theology fascinated me. Ideas that had been germinating in my mind for years began to crystalize. New scientific theories gave credence to some of my theological conclusions. My enthusiasm grew to the point where I wanted to test the ideas against the opinions of a large and diversified group of people. I thought, what better way to do this than to write a book on the subject.

Even though my field of scientific study has been in medicine I've done substantial reading in cosmology, non-Euclidean geometry, theoretical physics, logic and the scientific method. Logic, pure thought and a study of the Bible brought me to the conclusions that 1) time, as we understand it, is an illusion and 2) physical objects don't move. But I needed some authoritative source to either confirm or rebut my ideas.

In January 2000 a friend showed me a brief article from the New York Times about a book by Oxford physicist **Julian Barbour** titled, *The End Of Time, The Next Revolution in Physics*, published by Oxford Press. The thesis of this book is that 'time' is an illusion and physical objects don't move. Furthermore **Dr. Fred Allen Wolf**, a theoretical physicist from University of California, Los Angeles agrees. In his book *Parallel Universes* he states, "Nothing moving, nothing standing still." This is the paradoxical universe of space-time. These books explore some of the concepts I've wrestled with for years.

Telling the average person that time and motion are an illusion no doubt sounds absurd, but I have explained my reasoning to dozens of people of various ages, educational and socio-economic levels and no one has proved me wrong. A university physics professor told me my ideas were "hogwash," but another college professor of philosophy and logic found no fault with my reasoning. A marine architect commented that my ideas were not only fascinating but sounded plausible. My twelve-year-old grandson understood the concepts perfectly, and a fellow physician said my ideas were the most interesting he'd ever heard.

Dr. Hugh Ross, an evangelical minister and scientist with a Ph.D. in astrophysics from the University of Toronto, has written books on the cosmos, creation and evolution that have confirmed much of my thinking.

"Why waste time on such fanciful ideas? What's in it for me?" one might ask.

The answer is simple. These ideas open up an understanding of the Scriptures that are impossible to comprehend in any other way. **This is not science fiction**. We will see God and eternity without the encumbrances of clocks and calendars. We will explore miracles, death, the world of the occult and heaven as a place of physical reality.

This is a book for those who are looking for an intellectual adventure. It will stretch your imagination to the limits, yet I will give sound scientific and Biblical reasons for my assumptions. The ideas I'll set forth will expand your horizon of eternal events to an incredible degree. It will give you new insights into difficult scriptures that are usually considered allegorical, but are actually brilliant pictures of heavenly reality. We will proceed through a series of simple, logical steps, using non-technical language, based on accepted scientific and Biblical principles that will help you understand the inconceivable, see the invisible and believe the impossible. I will explain how logic and pure thought can accomplish this.

Don't be frightened by these statements. Much of the book consists of personal and fictional stories that illustrate these concepts, thereby making it more interesting and more easily understood.

For over fifty years, I have wrestled with these ideas. The conclusions have been so exciting that I want others to share in the knowledge of such remarkable possibilities; therefore, I invite you to accompany me on an intellectual pilgrimage of high adventure into the arcane world of the new theories of time and space.

Chapter One

Journey Into The Unknown

We hurtled through the blackness of the night at seventy miles an hour. There was no moon, no stars, only the bouncing headlights of the old Volkswagen to illuminate the winding narrow road. I was squeezed between two strangers in the back seat. The driver and the passenger in the front seat were engaged in lively conversation in a language I didn't understand. My two companions in the back seat were silent. I knew nothing about any of the passengers except for the one next to the driver, and I'd only met him the day before. He said he was a lawyer from Argentina. I'd met him on a train from Madrid to Brussels.

I happened to board the wrong train and the conductor was very upset and yelling at me in his native language. I had no idea what he was saying, and none of the visible passengers seemed to be paying any attention to our altercation.

Finally, a young man got up and approached the conductor. They conversed for a few minutes in his native tongue; then he turned to me and said, "You're on the wrong train, and even though you're going to the right destination your ticket is no good on this train. This is a local train and your ticket is for the express."

"Well, what am I supposed to do?" I asked.

Another conversation ensued between the conductor and the stranger.

Eventually the man turned to me and said, " The conductor has agreed to let you stay on this train."

The lawyer was proficient in English and I thanked him for his intervention. I sat with him the rest of the trip never dreaming it would lead to an experience of high anxiety.

When we arrived in Brussels I invited him to have dinner with me at my hotel. When we finished dinner and he was leaving he said, "Tomorrow night I'm going with some friends to a wonderful restaurant in a little town in the hill country. It's famous among the natives, but few tourists know about it. I would like you to go along if you are able."

I agreed, and here I am squeezed into a Volkswagen bug with total strangers, alone in a foreign country, headed for an unknown destination through the blackness of night at breakneck speed.

An hour went by. We passed through dimly lit towns with deserted streets, with no indication we were approaching the illusive restaurant.

My imagination began running wild. Who were these men and where were they taking me? Was there really a fascinating native meal awaiting me, or something else much more sinister? I began to wonder if I was too naive and had made a horrible mistake. I couldn't do much about it now, so I said a prayer and trusted the Lord as I have done so many times in the past.

Half an hour later we pulled up to the curb in another one of those little towns with dark, deserted streets.

"We're here," my host said.

I looked around, there was no sign of life, no other cars, or lighted buildings. We approached a store like structure with heavy curtains over its windows. He opened the door and a bright splash of light spilled out into the darkness.

Inside the tables were packed with a jovial crowd of local patrons. Because we had reservations we were seated immediately at our table. There was no menu, but before I could inquire about ordering, a huge platter of cooked fresh water shrimp, a large loaf of homemade peasant bread and several bottles of Vino Verde, a wine that is made from local wild green grapes, was placed on our table. I gorged on the shrimp and bread, listened to the local peasant music and thoroughly enjoyed the ambiance of another culture.

This adventure reminds me of the anxiety I feel when a stranger invites me to accompany him to a place with which I'm unfamiliar. There are similarities to my journey in Belgium and the one I'm inviting you to take with me. I'm asking you to travel with me into the unknown country of higher-dimensions of time and space, governed by the laws of theoretical physics, logic and abstract thinking. The things we will talk about will be discussed in everyday language, not scientific jargon.

Albert Einstein and many other eminent scientists have concluded that 'time', as we perceive it, is an illusion. The Bible tells us our concept of time is a distortion of eternal reality. *"For a thousand years in your sight are like a day that has just gone by, or like a watch in the night."* **Psalms 90:4**

As we look around us, we don't see the world as God created it. What we see is the beauty of God's creation distorted by sin, plagued by death, and groaning for the same redemption that we as Christians look foreword to. *"For the creation was subjected to frustration, not by its own choice, but by the will of the one who subjected it, in hope that the creation itself will be liberated from its bondage to decay and brought into the glorious freedom of the children of God. We know that the whole creation has been groaning as in the pains of childbirth right up to the present time."* ***Romans 8:20 – 22***

The time-space plane on which we live is a shambles of pain, sickness, sorrow and death. We look at it in the immediate 'NOW' of the present. We know only that which is in the realm of our five senses. We are unable to comprehend the destructive effect on the environment, past, present and future, brought on by the total depravity of mankind.

I hope to paint a picture for you that will give you a totally different concept of the state our world is in. I want you to see the five dimensional time-space plane in its entirety, as I envision God's seeing it. In the eyes of God, and according to some of the new theories of modern physics, the evil deeds of the past are still physically being perpetrated. Not only are plant, animal and human life suffering from this evil, but the earth and atmosphere as well.

Many scientists think they can find the solution to our problems by social, psychological and physical research. Furthermore, they believe they can do this without God. Some of them say there is no God, others say "Keep religion out of the schools, God has no place in science or edu-

cation." Morality is relative, prayer is no more than a superstitious remanent from our primitive past. But *"The One
enthroned in heaven laughs; the Lord scoffs at them. Then
he rebukes them in his anger and terrifies them in his
wrath." **Psalms 2:4-5**

Because our minds are controlled by 'three-dimensional
perception' we are missing the fantastic possibilities of
seeing time and eternity in their divine magnificence as depicted in the Scriptures. I want to awaken your imagination
and give you a glimpse of eternal reality.

Last night I turned on my TV. The movie *"Contact"* was
on; the science fiction creation of Carl Sagan, famous as-
tronomer and science writer. The story concerns a woman
scientist who is trying to contact intelligent life in outer
space. She receives a message from Vega, the planet of a
distant star. In the movie the characters talk about hyperspace, wormholes, time warps and aberrations of Time.
Although not a religious man, Carl Sagan, an eminent scientist, fantasized a fictional scientific scenerio that has very
important Biblical applications. You, too, will be exploring
some of these same fascinating possibilities as we take an
imaginary journey into the arcane world of time-space
travel. There is more reality to this fiction than most people
realize.

There is also a tangible world of occult reality of which
we must be aware if we are to escape the tentacles that
would drag us down to hell. **Science is based on the assumption that if a theory is not amenable to objective
testing, repetitive verification and independent confirmation it should not be trusted.** This is a valid requirement
for physical science, but there is an entire world of holistic
reality including the Christian Faith to which those
guidelines do not apply.

Scientists are reductionists; they think they can find
reality by dividing things into smaller and smaller units. As
one wag put it; "They learn more and more about less and
less until they finally know everything there is to know
about nothing at all". They can tell us everything about the

design, structure and operation of the universe, but they say nothing about the information it's transmitting from the God who created it. What they are telling us are true lies.

Atheistic physicians say when you die there is no continuing spirit. You are no better off than a bug smashed on the windshield of your car. They ignore the building body of evidence of life after death. The materialist scoffs at the thought of supernatural or metaphysical reality, but substantial research is being done in some of the most prestigious universities of the world relating to metaphysical phenomena that are inexplicable by conventional science.

It's interesting to note that it's not the theologians who are proving the Bible to be accurate, it's the secular scientists. Scientists are human, and like all humans they feel most comfortable when functioning within the framework of their accepted philosophy. For many of them, this is an a-priori assumption that every natural phenomenon can eventually be explained without resorting to a supernatural cause for its origin. They are afraid to venture into the unknown. They are like a man who wants to go fishing in a lake. He gets into the boat, takes the oars and starts to row, but he doesn't get very far because he is afraid to untie the boat from the wharf. His training ties him to the wharf of conventional natural science and he is unwilling to launch out into the vast unexplored depths of spiritual reality where the big trophies of truth can be caught.

There is no way to argue with this stand, because if they don't recognize the possibility of spiritual reality associated with the intelligent design of the universe they've negated any evidence that it exists. Some scientists will go to extremes to avoid considering divine involvement in natural phenomena. An example of this is the latest "origin of life" theory. When faced with the problem that the environmental conditions and age of the universe are inconsistent with their theories about the spontaneous development of life on earth, they often postulate solutions that are much less credible than the Biblical accounts of what happened. One of the latest theories of the origin of life on this earth is the theory of transpermia. This theory proposes that an intelligent source somewhere in the far reaches of the universe seeded the earth with living organisms. This begs the question. Where did that life come from? They're getting perilously close to the Biblical account.

The Bible tells us of a civilization in another universe, one inhabited by humans and other extraterrestrial beings. A universe not marred by sin and selfishness. We'll visit this universe in our imagination, but first we must understand parameters of reality that exist in such a place. Time in such a universe is much different than that which we experience here on earth. We will discover that objects have a fourth dimension and motion is also different than we perceive it on earth.

Few people realize these concepts are described in the Bible and that it has only been recently that science has given us the key to understand them. The trip will be an exciting intellectual experience so join me as we travel into the arcane world of hyperdimensional time and space.

Chapter Two
It's Time...To Understand

June 6 1944

Out of the twilight mists it came, so innocent in its appearance, so lethal in its mission, just like the sin that so easily beguiles us. It was a German Luftwaffe fighter-bomber with American markings. Standing on the deck of our LST (Landing Ship Tank) a hundred yards off Omaha Beach, I watched as the plane suddenly went into a power dive toward our starboard side. It banked, and three bombs floated silently toward our ship. Time stood still as the possibilities of what was about to happen flashed through my mind. Below deck tons of high explosives waited for the cue to do their work.

Time began to move again with paralyzing slowness. What would be next? My soul stripped of its flesh and left as a naked spirit on the bloody shores of Normandy?

There were three deafening blasts; geysers of water spurted skyward, but the bombs missed their target and our ship remained intact. Those few seconds seemed like hours. They stand out in my memory as occupying a huge segment of the time that I spent on Omaha Beach. In another setting the reverse was true.

I parked my car on a lonely road in the Berkeley Hills. The moon was bright and soft music from the car radio floated through the cool night air. The sparkling lights of the San Francisco Bay area spread out like a carpet of diamonds below us and in my arms was the woman I loved and would eventually marry.

Time fled in the fear of disrupting such precious moments. Hours flew by and it was time to take her home. How could it be? It seemed that only minutes had passed.

What is time?

The time-space plane on which we live, is a five dimensional time-space landscape cluttered by what we perceive to be a vast array of three dimensional objects and activities. We are time-space flatlanders and although there is a vertical time-space dimension we are unable to perceive it except intellectually. Ptolemy said it's impossible for the human mind to visualize higher dimensions. Evidence for the vertical dimension in time is assumed when one considers the existence of parallel universes floating above or below our universe. This concept has fascinating theological implications in relationship to Biblical doctrines of heaven, hell and eternity.

Time and space cannot be separated. If you have one you must have the other. In astro-physics scientists use the concept of time-space to measure stellar distances; as for us earthlings, we are prisoners of time. We walk through life blindfolded to the reality that surrounds us, comprehending only what we experience with our five senses in the immediate present. We can see nothing that's ahead of us, nothing in the present outside the range of our senses and we have only memories of what has gone before. We think the past is gone and the future hasn't occurred. That's the parochial theory of time. Science has a much more sophisticated concept, and Scripture confirms that the scientific concept of time is more compatible with the way God looks at things than the traditional way we look at them. It is for that reason I want you to understand the scientific view. The things we are going to talk about will be understood much more easily if you understand time in the framework of a scientific time-space model.

Time, as we experience it, is nothing more than a linear measurement on the five dimensional time-space plane where we live. An analogy comparing the three dimensions of space to the three dimensions of time-space may help you to conceptualize the model.

A simple diagram of dimensions one, two and three will help you understand the concept.

Figure One

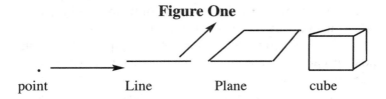

point   Line   Plane   cube

A point extended away from itself forms a line
A line extended at right angles to itself forms a plane
A plane extended at right angles to itself forms a solid

Figure Two

A single fourth dimensional cube measured in units of time from past to future

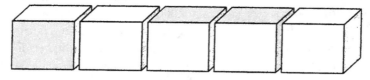

The fourth dimensional length is measured in units of time.
PAST   PRESENT   FUTURE

A three dimensional object can be extended at right angles to itself giving it a physical fourth dimension representing its existence from the time it first assumed its identity to the time when that identity was lost. It is not a series of three dimensional objects as depicted above but it's a single long physical object that manifests its shape to us at any moment in time as three dimensional. We are unable to visualize four dimensions.

Now let's do the same thing with time that we did above. A 'point' on the fourth dimensional time line has no fourth dimensional measurement, but once you make a 'point' it begins its progress through time and becomes a time line. There can be an infinite number of time lines in space lateral to one another and if there is a three dimensional object on each time line they are lateral to one another and that laterality in time creates a time-space plane.

If we take the five dimensional time-space plane and extend it in a vertical direction we have a time-space solid and in that solid an infinite number of time-space planes can exist, because a plane has no thickness. Furthermore, two time-space planes consisting of five dimensions each can be very close to each other and not be perceptible to an intelligent being on either plane.

In astro-physics a five dimensional time-space plane universe coexisting with our universe sometimes is considered a parallel universe, or a mirror universe. A parallel universe can be closer than two pages in a book with five dimensional physical objects just as real as those on earth, and be imperceptible to the human sensory system.

Recently there has been some interesting speculation in the scientific literature about higher dimensions. An article in *Scientific American* (August 2000) titled *The Universe's Unseen Dimensions*, starts out by saying, "The visible universe could lie on a membrane floating within a higher dimensional space."[1] If our flat universe is floating in a higher dimension, it would support the concept that the higher dimension in which it's floating is a dimension vertical to our flat time-space universe, indicating our universe is floating in a six dimensional time-space expanse[2].

We have just seen that a point in time has no temporal length. We might call that point "NOW". "NOW" is the time when we perceive whatever our five senses and our mind and thoughts tell us is the present, but "NOW" is never with us, for by the time we perceive it, NOW is already in the past. Life is an infinite number of "NOWs" strung out in a line running from the past into the future.

Are the past "NOWs" still there, or have they dissolved into nothingness? And are the future "NOWs" already in place, or do they materialize moment by moment as we step into the future?

For example, I have a giant redwood tree in my yard. It's at least one hundred and fifty years old. Is the tree still phys-

---

[1] Scientific American, August 2000 The Universes Unseen Dimensions by Nima Arkani-Hamed, Savas Dimopoulos and Georgi Dvali

[2] News article, Daily Republic, April 27,2000

ically present in the "NOW" of yesterday, ... or in the "NOW" of a hundred years ago? Are you also still physically present in the "NOW" of the years when you were a baby?

And if the tree isn't cut down, is it already physically there in the "NOW" of tomorrow, next week, and next year, ...or already in the "NOW" a thousand years hence? And what about you? Are you already there in the "NOW" of the ending years of your life and just haven't traveled that far along the time-space line?

Silly questions? Not really, because the answer to these questions is "yes" you are still physically present in the years gone by, and that answer is supported by the theories of science.[3] The early philosophers wrestled with these questions. Although they didn't understand "time" in the framework of modern science they recognized the implications. The early Greek thinkers believed in the absolute power of the forces of the universe and that man's destiny is determined by those powers. Heraclitus held that all change is in accordance with fixed and unalterable law. Zeno and the Stoics believed that everything in the universe is determined with an absoluteness that permits no break. Saint Augustine believed the passage of time began when Adam sinned, and the passage of time was the sentence of death for all living creatures. I agree. The Bible says, *"Therefore, just as sin entered the world through one man, and death through sin, and in this way death came to all men, because all sinned."* **Romans 5:12** Time is a wave of destruction that sweeps us toward death. It robs us of those lingering moments of bliss. It binds us to the slavery of the demands of the day. It creates a longing for the things of tomorrow. Because of Adam and Eve's sin man lost his freedom to choose, not only for himself, but also for all mankind. Now only God can decide who is worthy of salvation.[4]

The problem with all these philosophers is that they failed to grasp the concept that mankind has already exercised his free will, made his decisions, and the

[3] Wolf: Parallel Universes p.120

[4] Basic Teachings of the Great Philosophers

consequences have already occurred. With God there is no past, present and future. All of life is in the eternal present, and Einstein agrees. "People like us, who believe in physics, know that the distinction between past present and future is only a stubbornly persistent illusion."[5]

Furthermore, any change that occurs can only come to pass by the grace of God. In the eyes of God and in the eyes of science, our past present and future is nothing more than an eternal present, all of which is visible at the same time from a hyper dimensional point of view. **C.S Lewis**, in his book *Mere Christianity* says that God views our lives as a timeless entity, not as a series of daily events. This raises some profound theological questions.

Scientists have accepted the fact that time is a fourth spatial dimension. This implies all physical objects, including people, have a physical presence in the past and in the future. A dimension that measures their substance from the time they are first identified as a person until the time that identification no longer applies.

Let's use an example. You bake a loaf of bread at noon. When you take it out of the oven, you measure it. It's ten inches long by five inches wide and six inches high. But that's not all; it also has another measurement. At dinnertime it's physically seven hours long in its fourth temporal dimension. It was identified as a loaf of bread when you put in the oven at noon and it was completely eaten by 7:00 P.M.. It isn't a series of loaves of bread over those seven hours. It is physically one loaf of bread with a longitudinal temporal dimension of seven hours. It's impossible for us to see the loaf of bread in its higher dimensions because of the limitation of our five senses; however, logic tells us the fourth dimension must exist.

You may ask, "So what? I still have to get up at 6:30 A.M. in the morning and go to work. I come home at 5:30 P.M., eat dinner, watch TV and go to bed. 'Time' is absolute as far as I'm concerned. What difference do higher dimensions make?"

---

[5] p.232 hyperspace

First of all we should use a Biblical concept to understand what time is really like from God's point of view. The following verses give us a clue. *"For a thousand years in your sight are like a day that has just gone by, or like a watch in the night."* **Psalms 90:4** *"But do not forget this one thing, dear friends: With the Lord a day is like a thousand years, and a thousand years are like a day."* **2 Peter 3:8**

God wants us to live in the "NOW" of our relationship with Him." *This is the day the LORD has made; let us rejoice and be glad in it."* **Psalms 118:24** *"Therefore do not worry about tomorrow, for tomorrow will worry about itself. Each day has enough trouble of its own."* **Matthew 6:34**

We are continually saying to God, "I don't have time, ... to go visit that sick person,...to teach Sunday school, to attend the Bible study class,...to have my devotions today." By saying this, we are missing the greatest privilege given to mankind. We are missing the intimate companionship and communion with the creator of the universe. Paul instructs us to "P*ray continually; give thanks in all circumstances, for this is God's will for you in Christ Jesus."* **1 Thessalonians 5:17-18** To some that may seem impossible, or at least unrealistic, but dear friends it's imperative. Let me tell you a story.

✦   ✦   ✦   ✦   ✦

It was just the children's sermon, but I sat there silently in the uncomfortable awareness that the message was especially for me. I watched as the minister continued to drop the marbles into the glass. Each one representing the pressing tasks that faced me every day; marbles for the chores at home, a handful for the duties at work, more for my social responsibilities. The glass was full and marbles were spilling over the edge.

"You see, children, almost everyone's life is full of activities they consider important. At the end of the day, they say to themselves, 'I haven't had time to pray today, I'll try and do better tomorrow.'"

Then he took another glass filled with water. Carefully he poured the water over the marbles. The glass with the marbles was still able to hold almost a third of the water in the glass. In addition, every marble was surrounded by water. He continued, "Water represents the Holy Spirit, and each task will be accomplished more successfully if it is bathed in the Holy Spirit by a life filled with prayer. There is lots of room in everyone's life for communication with God."

Over the years, I've learned the meaning of this verse. People have interpreted it in a variety of ways; there are those who have gone to the seclusion of a monastery so they could devote all their time to meditation and prayer. Others continually repeat prayers associated with the beads of the rosary. Some Tibetans, when praying to Buddha write prayers on a drum called *"prayer wheels"* and spin them day in and day out. This is not what God is telling us to do when He tells us to pray without ceasing. In fact the Bible says, *"And when you pray, do not keep on babbling like pagans, for they think they will be heard because of their many words. Do not be like them, for your Father knows what you need before you ask him." **Matthew 6:7-8***

For the busy Christian with family responsibilities, a full time job and the crush of paying bills, going to meetings, keeping the house in repair and squeezing in a few hours of recreation, it seems there isn't much time for even a brief prayer, much less this business of praying all the time.

Before going into detail about "praying without ceasing," let us discuss some other things about our prayer life; why do we pray? Is it so God will know what we want? I don't think so, He already knows. *"—before they call, I will answer; and while they are yet speaking, I will hear." **Isaiah 65:24*** Prayer is not for God's benefit, but for ours. God wants us to petition him, praise him, intercede for others and meditate on our relationship with Him so we will keep in mind the unique relationship we enjoy by being his children.

There are several kinds of prayer and each kind contributes to the enrichment of our spiritual life, but they are different from the recommendation the apostle Paul is making in Thessalonians when he tells us to pray without ceasing. There are formal prayers, like the Lord's Prayer, and prayers written by famous scholars and theologians that are printed in prayer books and hymnals. The grandeur of some of these prayers inspires and blesses the supplicant beyond anything he/she can compose, but they are not meant to be repeated to one's-self ad infinitum.

Then there are public prayers. Prayer that is more for the benefit of other listeners than for the one doing the praying. Certainly one is not going to go around all day praying out loud. Next there is the prayer of private devotions, when one's entire focus is on a personal relationship with God. In these prayers are elements of thankfulness, praise and petition. But again, this entails shutting out world and its distracting influences, and they are not practical for twenty-four hour a day use. Many people engage in prayer of prolonged meditation whereby communication with God is established by mood and attitude rather than by words. This is more suitable for special occasions or for the monk in a monastery. A mature Christian will find that there are times when a period of intercessory prayer is necessary for some very special person or need. These types of prayer have a place in our lives, but none is suited to the admonition to pray without ceasing. There is a kind of prayer that does fit the criteria of Paul's admonition; I refer to it as conversational prayer. It's a wonderful, exciting and rewarding experience.

When walking with a loved one it's not necessary to communicate with that person by talking all the time. I remember walking with my wife, when for long periods not a word was exchanged, but the warmth of her hand in mine, her occasional glance, the aura of her presence, was a communication between us that exceeded the ability of words to describe. When an appropriate thought came to mind, or when something special in our environment attracted our attention, we would express it in words. That's the way we should walk with God, every minute of every day.

Do you genuinely thank God when you find a good place to park your car? When you look at the green hills and the fluffy clouds, do you spontaneously say, "Thank you Lord for the beautiful world you gave us to live in happily and peacefully?" If someone cuts you off in traffic, or steals the parking place you were about to pull into, do you ask the Lord to bless them? The Bible says, *"But I tell you: Love your enemies and pray for those who persecute you."* **Matthew 5:44** Do you pray for the beggar on the street, the child that catches your attention on the playground, or the man being arrested by the police? Do you perform random acts of kindness that are accompanied by a prayer?

One of the important things about this kind of prayer is to allow time for God to talk to you. The way you do this is by quoting Scripture you have memorized. I live in a location surrounded by hills and mountains. When I go out to get the paper in the morning, I look at the gorgeous terrain and repeat **Psalms 121** *"I lift up my eyes to the hills— where does my help come from? My help comes from the LORD, the Maker of heaven and earth."* What an inspiring way to start the day. At night, when I look up at the heavens, the deep purple of the sky and the myriad stars, the words of the **Psalms 8** surge into my mind. *"When I consider your heavens, the work of your fingers, the moon and the stars, which you have set in place, what is man that you are mindful of him, the son of man that you care for him? You made him a little lower than the heavenly beings and crowned him with glory and honor."* **Psalms 8:3-5** When it's time to sleep, my conversation with God continues with **Psalms 63:6** *"On my bed I remember you; I think of you through the watches of the night."* This is especially appropriate when I awake in the middle of the night and am unable to go back to sleep. For me, praying is as effective as a sleeping pill. The reassurance that, *"And he who searches our hearts knows the mind of the Spirit, because the Spirit intercedes for the saints in accordance with God's will. And we know that in all things God works for the good of those who love him, who have been called according to his purpose."* **Romans 8:27-28**   *"I will lie down and sleep in peace, for you alone, O LORD, make me dwell in safety."*

Psalms 4:8   With those thoughts I doze off in the arms of my loving Father, and *"When I awake (He says) I am still with you." Psalms 139:18*

When troubling or inappropriate thoughts start crowding into my mind? I rely on *2 Corinthians 10:4 "The weapons we fight with are not the weapons of the world. On the contrary, they have divine power to demolish strongholds. We demolish arguments and every pretension that sets itself up against the knowledge of God, and we take captive every thought to make it obedient to Christ."* When things aren't going well, even after I have prayed about them, I remember *Romans 8:28 "And we know that in all things God works for the good of those who love him, who have been called according to his purpose."* A dozen times a day verses of praise, comfort, support and petition come to mind in appropriate situations.

There is no substitute for memorizing God's Word. Many Christians stumble through life, spending a few minutes from time to time saying a short prayer; they barely know anything about the tremendous resources that are at their disposal. They remind me of the situation I am in with my computer. I use my computer mainly for word processing, but the vast resources I have available in my software programs and on the Internet boggle my mind. I have at my disposal the resources to access fantastic information, but I don't know how to take advantage of much of what is available to me. Many Christians are in the same position. The resources that are available from a thorough knowledge and application of the scriptures are beyond their comprehension. The more you read the book of instructions (the Bible), the more you will hear God talking to you and appreciate the power of the resource He has given you.

God speaks to us in many ways, but none are more specific than what is written in His Holy Word. When you pray without ceasing, it is essential you not do all the talking. Enhance God's communication with you by storing in your mind as much scripture as possible. Then you really can experience the joy of praying without ceasing.

The apostle John says, **John 8:32** *"Then you will know the truth, and the truth will set you free."* The 'truth' is that as sinners we are prisoners of time and when we are born again we have been given eternal life and are living in a "NOW" relationship with God. No longer do we have to let time control our relationship with God. We can pray without ceasing. When you understand higher dimensions you see things and events from God's perspective. This can make a significant difference in what you believe and the way you live.

Chapter Three
Nothing Moves,
Nothing Changes

If I tell you the motion of physical objects is an illusion, you'll think I'm off my rocker. You stand by a freeway and you see cars flying by at seventy miles an hour; you watch the Navy's Blue Angels dart, dive and swirl against a clear blue sky; you get on a roller coaster and feel your heart come up in your throat when the car drops out from under you as you plummet down the first steep grade, but the new physics says nothing moves.

I'm not sure it's entirely true that nothing moves, but generally speaking most of the objects you think are moving are stationary. When sin entered into the world, the entire time-space plane that we live on changed, and froze into a cruel, twisted, deformed, landscape, from its beginning in time to the end of history. **C.S. Lewis** in the *Tales of Narnia* tells of a similar event when Edward eats the forbidden 'Turkish Delight' and the White Witch turns him into a statue to join the many other immobile victims of her evil power. Humanity became a prisoner of time and all motion stopped. Only the passage of time gives the illusion of motion as it propels us toward an inevitable death that has already occurred. The Bible says we are already dead. *"And if Christ be in you, the body is dead because of sin; but the Spirit is life because of righteousness."* **Romans 8:10** I believe there is adequate evidence to conclude the world and the unsaved in the world have lost their free will. They are traveling an irrevocable, motionless course through time and space over which they have no control. On the other hand, the redeemed have regained their free will, and with it a limited degree of motion. *"Then you will know the truth, and* *the truth will set you free*." ***John 8:32*** It is because of this freedom we are able to exercise our free will and learn obedience to God.

As previously stated, **Julian Barbour**, in his recent book, *The End of Time, The Next Revolution in Physics*, proposes that the popular concept of motion is an illusion. The idea that the passage of time is an illusion has been around for quite awhile, but the idea that motion is an illusion is a radical idea and it impacts the validity of what we consider to be the reality of everyday observation, as well as many of the conventional laws of classical physics. In spite of the fact we are surrounded by what we interpret to be objects in motion the logic of this new theory is inescapable, especially as it relates to a Biblical idea of God's view of us as individuals. The story I'm about to tell you of an experience I had with objects that were perceived to be in motion, is an example of how I, as a Christian, exercised my free will to decide between two options God placed before me, and how that decision altered the course of my life. I don't believe the non-Christian would have had this option.

✦   ✦   ✦   ✦   ✦

There was an exhilarating bite in the frigid night air. The dull glow of gas street lamps danced on the glistening white of the packed snow that covered the streets. It was December 22, 1929 and my best friend, Gordon and I were selling Christmas trees in front of my parents' Bible School at 25th Street and Maryland Avenue in Baltimore, Maryland. Business was slow and the five block long hill stretching before us was deserted.

My Flexible Flyer sled, leaning against the fence, presented an irresistible temptation to take a long exciting ride down the empty street. Little did I realize that yielding to this temptation would completely change my life, and my life needed changing. I'm a preacher's kid and I was saturated with evangelical truth intellectually, but my behavior and interests did not reflect the loving teaching to which I was constantly exposed. I was surreptitiously smoking and thinking more about having fun and making money than listening to God speaking to me about His plan for my life. I didn't realize God is not easily put off, and I'm sure the event about to occur was planned and essentially already in place.

While Gordon and I were debating who would take the first ride a friend of ours stopped by and enquired, "How's business?"

Gordon's face lit up. "Slow," he answered. "How about watching the business while Bill and I take a short ride?"

"Okay," he answered.

Gordon Picked up the sled and said, "Bill, lets do a double decker. I'll get us started and you belly-flop on top of me."

He ran a half dozen steps and flopped on the sled. Within seconds I was on top of my friend and we were speeding down the hill. The polished steel runners sang as they glided over the smooth, hard snow-pack. We were gathering speed as we crossed the first intersection. The second intersection flew past. As we cleared the third intersection, a taxicab turned in behind us. The cab had only cowl lights, but surely he would see us, — I was wrong. A quick look over my shoulder indicated the taxi was slowly overtaking our speeding sled. There seemed to be no escape. A four-foot snow bank was on one side of us and on the other side, streetcar tracks. The cab inexorably closed the distance between us.

I grasped Gordon more tightly. If we could just make it to the next intersection he would have room to turn into the cross street and we would avoid being hit by the taxi...I thought.

Again I looked over my shoulder. To my horror all I could see was the front end of the cab. It towered above us like a gigantic animal ready to attack.

Then the inevitable happened. The front wheel hit us and spun the sled around in a cloud of ice and snow. I felt a dull crunch as the wheels went over both my legs that were still

on top of Gordon. The world spun like a surrealistic merry-
go-round. Finally the spinning stopped and the foreboding
chill of the darkened street gave a ghastly reality to what had
just happened.

I looked around. My friend Gordon lay sprawled on the
ice a few feet away, face down and not moving.

The cab stopped and the driver and his passengers ran
back to the smashed sled and the two broken bodies lying in
the street.

Gordon rolled over and sat up.

"Are you all right?" the taxi passengers gasped.

"What a dumb question," I thought.

Instead of calling an ambulance the driver helped me to
my feet, and even though my right leg would not support my
weight I hobbled over to the cab. Gordon was able to walk
with help. They loaded us into the cab and the driver drove
us to the taxi-dispatching garage to arranged transportation
for the cab's passengers. He then proceeded to fill out an accident report.

The numbness and the shock of the accident began to
wear off and an agonizing pain enveloped my lower body.
Gordon was white as a sheet. Twenty minutes later the
driver finally finished his report and drove us to Maryland
General Hospital.

Emergency Room personnel recognized I was seriously
hurt. They put me on a gurney and rushed me into a
treatment room. We were both examined and x-rayed.
Gordon was not badly hurt. The wind had been knocked out
of him; he suffered severe bruises of the chest and he had a
fractured shoulder blade. I had a severe injury. X-rays
showed a severe crushing, comminuted fracture of my right
femur.

The Emergency Room doctor immediately put in a call
for the attending orthopedic surgeon and one of the nurses
called my parents. Within thirty minutes my father and
mother were by my side.

The doctor stunned my parents by saying, " He has a
badly comminuted fracture of his right femur, and he'll have

to have his right leg amputated as soon as our orthopedic surgeon arrives." (At that time immediate amputation was a common procedure for my type of fracture, because people with that kind of injury had a high morbidity and mortality rate.)

My parents silently prayed that I might be spared this terrible procedure.

God does interesting things in answer to prayer. The orthopedic surgeon did not respond to the summons by the hospital and so I was put to bed on the surgical ward and scheduled for surgery in the morning.

(Later we were told, incredibly, that the orthopedic surgeon who would have amputated my right leg that night had, that very evening, developed a case of amnesia, wandered off and was not found for several days.) My parents thanked God for the delay. Finally they recovered from the shock of my accident and called our family pediatrician for advice.

"We must get him out of there at once," she said. " I'll call Dr. George Bennett. He's the Professor of orthopedic surgery at John Hopkins University Hospital and a world-renowned orthopedic surgeon. We'll have him transferred to his care."

Dr. Bennett agreed to accept me as a patient, and Maryland General Hospital was notified I was to be transferred the next morning to Dr. Bennett's service at Church Home and Infirmary, a satellite facility of John Hopkins Hospital.

The place where I would spend the night was an open surgical ward of twenty beds. By now it was midnight but a pounding pain in my leg made sleep impossible. From various parts of the ward, the stillness of the night was peppered with frequent unanswered calls of "Nurse, nurse." In the background the groans of a dying patient lent a macabre setting to a night I'll never forget. A gruff old man in the cubicle next to me sat on the edge of his bed chain smoking cigarettes and giving me the case histories of the patients sharing our ward About three A.M. the groaning of the dying man stopped. An orderly and a nurse appeared; a gurney was rolled in and about ten minutes later the gurney with a figure shrouded in a white sheet was rolled past my bed on the way to the morgue.

I hadn't cried up to that time, but as the dawn began to break tears welled up in my eyes and uncontrollable sobs shook my body. It wasn't from the pain; the entire nightmare of the past twelve hours finally overwhelmed me.

My ambulance trip to Church Home and Infirmary was a tremendous relief. On my arrival at the hospital, I was given a single room with cheerful amenities and put under the care of loving nurses.

For the next two weeks, I was in leg traction to correct the two-inch override of the fractured ends of the femur. And every day for two weeks Dr. Bennett would come in, put both thumbs on the end of the distal fragment of bone and push as hard as he could in an effort to realign the fracture site. The pain was agonizing, but I gritted my teeth, clenched the side rails of my bed and soaked the sheets with perspiration.

Finally, he conceded he was unable to accomplish re-alignment of the fractured bone and so I was scheduled for an open reduction of the fracture.

After performing extensive reconstructive surgery, using devices that he had invented and which bear his name today, he said to my parents, " The fracture site was a mess, but I was able to save his leg. He'll be in a body cast and he'll have to stay in the hospital for the next six weeks."

The six weeks went by like a wonderful dream. I got great meals, friends from our church sent candy, fruit and flowers and I had my own radio, a real treat in the early thirties. Then, one day the nurse came in and said, "Guess what? You're having your cast off today and in a few days you can go home."

I was ambivalent about the news. I'd gotten used to the hospital, I was in love with one of the nurses. (I thought) I was being treated like a king; but time and tide wait for no man. My cast was cut off and the stitches removed from my incision.

When I looked at my leg, it looked like a pole. The muscles were wasted, and I had no motion in my knee. Over the next few days, I was given lessons on the use of crutches. Finally, the day came for me to go home.

Three months before my accident our family doctor decided I had a heart condition and advised my parents that I not attend the fall semester of school. The stress of the accident took its toll. The symptoms that kept me out of school became worse.

I asked my father, an ordained minister, to anoint me with oil and pray for me in accordance with James 5:14. He did, but I didn't get better. I wondered why, and I was soon to find out.

It was Thursday evening; two weeks after my discharge from the hospital. I was short of breath and my heart was doing funny things. The doctor had come to see me at two o'clock that afternoon and left some medicine. The medicine wasn't working.

My mother sat beside my bed reading her Bible. Her face was drawn and her skin was ashen.

Feebly I said, "I think you better call the doctor again."

Although there was a phone by my bed she went downstairs to make the call. When she didn't return right away I became apprehensive. Quietly I lifted the bedside phone off its cradle and put it to my ear. I caught the doctor's last words as she said to my mother, "There is nothing more I can do. When the end comes, I'll come back and sign the certificate."

The year was 1930. There were no antibiotics, no sophisticated diagnostic procedures, no intensive care units. Medical science had done all it could for me without avail and I was going to die.

I was only fifteen. I didn't want to die; I had wonderful plans for my future. Ever since I was eight years old I'd wanted to go to the Naval Academy. There was salt water in my veins. My great, great grandfather was a privateer named Captain Boyle and a book had been written about him and his ship "The Lively Lady" by Kenneth Roberts. I dreamed of sailing to exotic ports and of having exciting adventures, but now those dreams were fading. I was going to die.

It was hard for me to breath. I took my pulse. It was 140 and barely perceptible.

I was in a state of panic. I looked at the bedside clock. It was 7:05 P.M.. I closed my eyes. How much longer would I live? My past floated through my mind. There was much of which I wasn't proud and for which I needed to ask for forgiveness. I felt God was telling me to trust Him: to give Him my life, my dreams, my future without reservation. I seemed to be slipping into unconsciousness. I closed my eyes and prayed, " Dear Father, forgive me for my selfish desires, I love you, I'm yours, all that I am, all that I have and all that I hope to be."

I didn't pray to be healed, or for my life to be spared. I just prayed for Him to put His arms around me and hold me close. I sensed no assurance I would live, but I could feel His love. I knew He loved me so much He sent His Son to die for my sins. He would be with me in death, or in life if He chose to let me live.

With the awareness of His love and forgiveness a billow of peace flowed over me. The anger, the stress and the panic that was killing me was gone and in the quietness that followed I could feel His presence. Again I looked at the bedside clock. It was 7:22 P.M. It had taken me seventeen minutes to fully surrender my life to God.

I was no longer afraid and I drifted off into a peaceful sleep not knowing if I would ever wake up.

It took four years for me to regain enough strength to return to school. By then, I knew God wanted me to be a doctor. God not only saved my leg by a miraculous coincident He also remembered my love of the sea. In medical school, I was commissioned an ensign in the U.S. Navy Reserve. Following graduation I was promoted to Lieutenant (j.g.) USN and ordered to active duty. During World War II, I had five years of active duty packed with excitement and service to my Lord and Savior. I discovered God's plan for my life was so much better than anything I'd dreamed of that there was no comparison.

It's my contention that I had the opportunity to exercise my free will to give up my selfish plans and trust God with my life and my future, or fight to live and try to hold on to those selfish dreams.

It's hard to comprehend how the event just described could be devoid of motion. I can still feel the sting of the bitter wind whipping across my face, and hear the crackle of the polished steel runners as my sled glided over the packed snow on the darkened street. The taxi surely was moving as it hungrily pursued our speeding sled and devoured it in a whirlwind of ice and snow, but in the eyes of God this entire drama was like a photograph of an event that had already happened. I had the opportunity to react to that event by the exercise of my free will. It was not a decision regarding my eternal salvation. It was a decision as to my willingness to submit to the plans God had for my life. I think if I hadn't fully trusted God in that circumstanceI I would still have been saved, but I might have died and events in my future would have been altered. Logic and science say the future physically exists. If science is right, and since God is outside our framework of time and space He sees the physical end and the physical beginning at the same time. In other words, God sees the future as a fact before it occurs in our perception.

Chapter Four
Creation And A Static Universe

God can do anything He wants to do, at any time and in any place. What He did for me the night I surrendered my life to Him I believe was accomplished before I was born. Furthermore, although this accident represented a crisis in my life I don't believe He disrupts the natural laws of the universe to respond to an emergency. With God there are no emergencies. He sees the past, present and future in one glance. The disturbing events we face in our daily life are designed by God to develop our faith in His infinite power and goodness.

Historically and personally we can see how God has worked to solve the problems of His children, but many scientists mock these events as imaginary, or as mere coincidences because they don't conform to their understanding of natural law.

In spite of their scoffing, paradoxically, they are developing theories giving scientific credibility to a mechanism for their occurrence. Hyperdimensional theory and new concepts of time and space have opened up avenues for the theological exploration of fantastic miracles.

Many years ago, on a visit to the Griffith Park Planetarium in Los Angeles, I saw an exhibit demonstrating the theory that the illusion of motion of physical objects is caused by the passage of time, not the movement of the object observed. It was a tall black box about two feet square and five and a half feet tall, it had a curtain in the front and it was open in the back. There was a slit in the curtain about one centimeter wide. On the side of the curtain opposite the slit was a handle. One could look through the slit, grasp the handle and pull it downward. As the slit moved downward one saw balls of light moving around each other in the same pattern the planets describe as they move around the sun. When the slit stops moving the balls of light stop moving.

When one walks around to the back of the box and looks in, all one sees is a series of lighted neon tubes twisted around each other. The slit is the same width as the diameter of the glass tubes making the glass tubes look like balls. Viewing the changing relationships of the tubes to one another, as seen through the moving slit, creates the illusion the balls of light are moving around each other.

Black Box: Griffith Park Planetarium

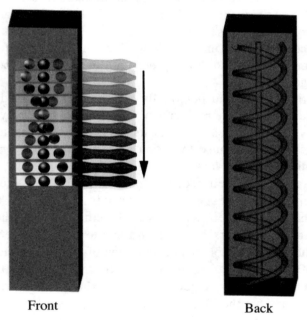

Front

Back

Figuire Three

*Drawing on the left labeled, **Front View of the Box**.*
*Drawing on the right labeled, **View of Back Side of the Box**.*
The drawing on the left side illustrates the changing relationship of the balls of light as the slit in the curtain progresses downward. The drawing on the right side show the twisted neon tubes in the box that create the illusion of moving balls of light.

The exhibit demonstrates the phenomenon we interpret, as the motion of objects may be an illusion. We observe the movement of time (the slit in the curtain) not the movement of objects. Forty or more years have passed since I saw this exhibit. The logic involved continues to impress me, even though it is contrary to the accepted laws of physics and common sense. As time passes, we see a change in the relationship of fourth dimensional physical objects to one another much like the tubes in the black box. The past and future of the objects is just as real as the three dimensional image of the present being seen as "NOW." Their temporal fourth dimension is static, but the passage of each moment gives a different picture of the relationship between two or more separate cross sections of the objects, giving the illusion of motion.

The following analogy may help. Assume that I'm walking along a road with a blindfold we shall call time. The blindfold totally occludes all visual perception of my environment. I use a cane to feel my way along the road. With my cane, I feel a rock and avoid being tripped; I touch a tree and avoid a collision. I'm warned of a ditch, a hill, a mud hole; —my world is interpreted as "NOW" solely by the cane in my hand (that represents my 5 senses). I'm unaware of the flowers by the road, the cattle grazing on the rolling hills, or the car speeding toward the intersection I'm about to cross. My perception is a prisoner of the blindfold, and my shackled senses limited to the cane in my hand. Then the blindfold is removed.

Now I can see where I'm going. I can see the paths on each side of me I could have taken, and the landscape I have already passed. In addition, I can look up and see the birds in the trees, the snow-capped mountains, the sunset, and the stars. My journey across the time-space plane becomes an entirely new and exciting adventure as I look ahead to what I'm about to experience.

The above analogy helped me visualize the possibilities of higher dimensions. Oxford physicist **Julian Barbour's**, *The End of Time, The Next Revolution in Physics* reinforced my ideas.

In addition to Barbour's theory about time and motion, this concept throws an entirely new light on the creation story. It offers a more logical alternative to the debatable assumptions about evolution. If we truly live in a static universe, then the past still exists on the time-space plane, and future development of various forms of life has already occurred. We just haven't reached them in our travel along the time-space road. Understanding this can shed light on the enigma of "twenty-four hour days" of creation.

The static universe theory completely unravels our parochial notions of God working by a clock that's ticking off minutes and hours. No passage of time exists with God. Furthermore, this theory implies that God created the entire five dimensional time-space universe from its beginning to its end and all the objects on it in their entirety exactly as the Bible states. For instance, in **Genesis: 1:11 and 12**: *"Then God said, Let the land produce vegetation: seed-bearing plants and trees on the land that bear fruit with seed in it, according to their various kinds." And it was* [instantaneously]{my insert} *so. **The land produced vegetation: plants bearing seed according to their kinds and trees bearing fruit** with seed in it according to their kinds. And God saw that it was good."*

This clearly states that the life cycle of plants and trees, from the moment of their creation to the end of time, were created instantaneously. They went through their growth cycles, had seeds and bore fruit from the beginning to the end of their existence, before the next day of creation took place.

My redwood tree was created and put in its position on the time-space plane exactly where it is now on the third day of creation. It is still in the "NOW" of the past when it was a seedling, and will be in the "NOW" of tomorrow. All plant life is present, as well as everything else, from the day of their creation to the day of their extinction.

This theory offers a logical alternative to Darwinian evolution, in that the ideas are based on theories of science as well as on Biblical references. If there is no passage of time with God when He created the universe, then there was no evolutionary development; He fashioned the universe, the world and all of life as six layered segments superimposed on top of each other; with each layer having a different linear time-space life span. The earlier layers having a linear time-space length consistent with the calculated geological ages, but each layer was created in its entirety from the beginning of time to the end of time.

Levels of Creation

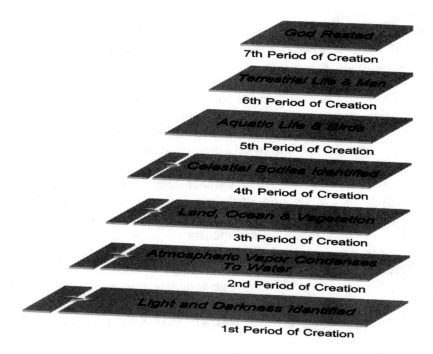

7th Period of Creation

6th Period of Creation

5th Period of Creation

4th Period of Creation

3th Period of Creation

2nd Period of Creation

1st Period of Creation

Figure Four

Each period of creation was completed in its entirety in a single instant, From its beginning to its end, before the next layer was created. e.g.: In the third period of creation the last bit of vegetation that will be present on the earth when the earth ceases to exist came into physical being at the same time the first bit of vegetation was created. All vegetation that ever existed or ever will exist was created at the same time.

From a standpoint of pure logic this must be. Otherwise, you are stuck with the illogical assumption that no physical objects exist in the future. In other words, the ground you are standing on is non-existent a nano-second in the "NOW" of the future. It's ridiculous to think that when you're driving down the highway at sixty miles an hour the road you're driving on is not already a factual reality in the future. Intellectually you know the road is still there in the past, because although you drove over it today, someone else is going to be driving over it tomorrow.

To fully understand this, we must remember these fundamental facts. Time is a human concept and has been shown to be an illusion by both science and the Bible (Einstein and **2 Peter 3:8**) Time-space is a five dimensional plane with two sides, a beginning point and an end margin. God is not constrained to work within the limits of time and space. From His perspective He can hear millions of prayers at once and devote unlimited attention to each individual, because for God time is not passing.

God is an artist of incomprehensible skill. One needs only to look at the glory of the sunsets, the lavish colors of equatorial birds and flowers, the amazing shape and color of tropical fish. From the macrocosm to the microcosm the beauty, precision and skill attest to the perfection of the creator.

Now, how would an artist go about creating such a masterpiece? First, he sets up a blank canvas, (**Genesis 1:1**) and then he determines which part will have a light and dark background.

An artist does not usually put in the minute details of a picture as he goes along. He first establishes a framework, then the broad outline of what is going to be the picture, and finally the detail.

When God created the universe He didn't have to worry about starting in the morning in order to accomplish a certain amount by bedtime. "*...even the darkness will not be dark to you; the night will shine like the day, for darkness is as light to you.*" **Psalms 139:12** God doesn't work by a time clock. The entire time-space plane spread out before Him as an eternal "NOW," and He filled in the details, as He desired.

As He created the universe, He did it in layers corresponding to the geologic record, from the Precambrian period to the Quaternary period. Each layer was laid down in its entirety from the beginning elements attesting to its identity to the end of time. God did not establish a time period for that segment of creation until after it was finished. I believe the statements, "the evening and the morning refer to the end of one segment and the beginning of the next.

The Bible tells us that in the beginning He put everything that is, was, or will be on the time-space plane. And all was in the present until Adam and Eve sinned. In other words, there was no past or future, no ticking clock, and no twenty-four hour days during creation. The passage of time did not begin until after Adam and Eve sinned. In God's eyes it was all "NOW", from the beginning of the time-space plane to the end of it. However this concept creates a dilemma that needs to be mentioned now.

When were we put on the time-space plane, and what about free will? The Bible says we were identified before the creation of the world. How do we know that our position on the time-space plane was determined before creation? Let us look at several scriptures that tell us.

From the assumptions that our salvation was determined before creation of the world, it may appear that I'm a predeterminist. If the past, present and future are fixed and unchangeable then where does free will come in? I believe that when we were given an identifiable personality; "a soul," we exercised our free will to either accept or reject Jesus Christ as our Savior. God permitted us total freedom to make this decision outside of time without interfering in the least with our free will. God did not predestine us to be saved or not saved. On the basis of His foreknowledge, He accepted us. Foreknowledge in no way hinders the exercise of our free will.

I have three adult children. Even with my limited human knowledge, I know what they will do when confronted with most situations. My knowing ahead of time how they will react to given circumstances does not impinge on their free will to chose. Foreknowledge does not imply controlling free will, but based on that foreknowledge I'm able to predict their behavior in various situations with a high degree of accuracy.

"And we know that in all things God works for the good of those who love him, who have been called according to his purpose. For those God foreknew he also predestined to be conformed to the likeness of his Son, that he might be the firstborn among many brothers. And those he predestined, he also called; those he called, he also justified; those he justified, he also glorified." **Romans 8:28-30**

Because of God's foreknowledge He knew what our behavior would be in various situations, *"For he chose us in him before the creation of the world to be holy and blameless in His sight. In love He predestined us to be adopted as his sons through Jesus Christ, in accordance with his pleasure and will."* **Ephesians 1:4-5** *"I pray for them. I am not praying for the world, but for those you have given me, for they are yours."* **John 17:9** *"Your eyes saw my unformed body. All the days ordained for me were written in your book before one of them came to be."* **Psalms 139:16**

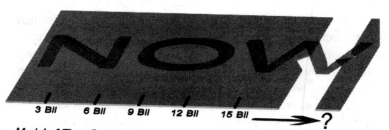

Model of Time-Space Plane Universe from it's Beginning to it's End

Figure Five

God sees our time-space plane from beginning to end always in the present, without past, present, or future. A billion years ago to us is still "NOW" in the eyes of God.

Before sin entered into the equation, the earth was an entirely different place. It was not static, and time was not pushing events forward as it does now. People and animals could move backward into the past, forward into the future or sideways along the time-space line of the present on the time-space plane. The environment was cooperative with human endeavor, and man lived in an eternal present "NOW". How long this went on we don't know because, even though mileposts across the time-space plane may have existed, there was no forced passage of time until sin became a factor. The basis for this is ***Genesis 3:16-19***.

To the woman He said, *"I will greatly increase your pains in childbearing; with pain you will give birth to children. Your desire will be for your husband, and he will rule over you."*

To Adam He said, *"Because you listened to your wife and ate from the tree about which I commanded you, 'You must not eat of it,'* "Cursed is the ground because of you; through painful toil you will eat of it all the days of your life. It will produce thorns and thistles for you, and you will eat the plants of the field."*

In my opinion, this was the beginning of the illusion of passing time, and the sentence of death.

"Therefore, just as sin entered the world through one man, and death through sin, and in this way death came to all men, because all sinned—Wherefore, as by one man sin entered into the world, and death by sin; and so death passed on all men, for that all have sinned: For until the law sin was in the world: but sin is not imputed when there is no law. Nevertheless death reigned from Adam to Moses, even over them that had not sinned after the similitude of Adam's transgression, who is the figure of him that was to come."
Romans 5:12-14

Chapter Five
Flat Land
The Journey Begins

Hyperdimensional reality is beyond the perceptive capability of our five senses. In order to give you a picture of the subject, rather than outline scientific theories and formulas, I'm going to take you on an imaginary journey to illustrate the concept and some of its implications.

✦　　✦　　✦　　✦　　✦

"Ladies and gentlemen, may I have your attention please." Her voice had a thick Hungarian accent. "Welcome to 'Timescape Explorer', the world's first passenger "time travel" machine. We're about to embark on an amazing adventure, and to appreciate what you're about to see you need to listen carefully as I explain the phenomena of space travel in higher dimensions.

Our captain for today's journey is Peter von Rock and our navigator is Joe Christian."

The voice was that of Trebla Nietsnie, famous Hungarian astro-physicist, now doing research at the International Time-Space Center at Los Alamos, New Mexico. Her azure gray eyes flashed with enthusiasm; her supple well-rounded body spoke of a rigid physical discipline complementing her razor sharp mind. There was a tautness of her muscles that resembled a greyhound about to start a race. But strangely, her infectious smile exuded a feeling of relaxation, and confidence. You could tell she was someone in authority who knew exactly what to do, and how to do it. With her in charge you would be safe.

She was standing at the hatchway of a beautifully built vehicle, made from super-galactic meteorite material found

only on Mars. Crafted by a consortium of scientists and engineers from all over the world it had speeds capable of
breaking the time-space barrier. To do this it had to
withstand nuclear, magnetic and gravitational forces beyond
anything that could be duplicated by materials found on
earth.

"The principle is very simple," she continued. "We all
are familiar with the three dimensional measurements of
space, but to understand time-travel it's necessary to visualize a hyperdimensional universe with three 'time'
dimensions added to the three familiar space dimensions.
The first pure dimension of time is referred to in scientific
literature, as the fourth dimension. The fourth dimension
represents the temporal length of a three dimensional
physical object from the time it's first identified as that
object until the time when it's identity is lost.

You've already been given a brochure on hyperdimensional time-space with diagrams and explanations, so I
won't bore you with needless repetition. I do want to review
a few of the basic concepts in order to make sure you understand what's happening as we take our journey.

Two time-space planes, similar to our universe, each consisting of five dimensions, can be very close to each other
and not be perceptible to an intelligent being on either time-
space plane. In astro-physics another five dimensional
time-space plane coexisting with our five dimensional
universe is sometimes considered a parallel universe, or a
mirror universe. In thinking back to Biblical times we find
the Hebrew concept of heaven is consistent with the modern
theory of a parallel universe. A separate universe closer than
two pages in a book, with solid, physical five dimensional
objects and people, just as real as those on earth, can be imperceptible to the human sensory system.

Recently there has been some interesting speculation in
the scientific literature about higher dimensions, and as
mentioned in your brochure, the article in Scientific
American (August 2000) titled The Universe's Unseen
Dimensions, starts out by saying, "The visible universe

could lie on a membrane floating within a higher dimensional space."[1] If our five dimensional universe is floating in a higher dimensional space, it could well be that another five dimensional universe in a vertical dimension of time-space is floating just above us, thus resulting in two or more flat five dimensional time-space universes floating in a six dimensional time-space expanse.[2] It becomes obvious that you can't have a five dimensional time-space plane floating in a geometric figure unless that figure has a vertical dimension.

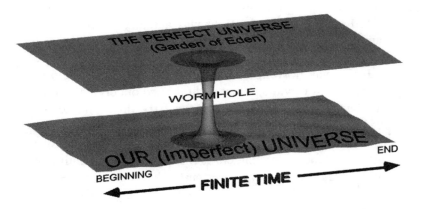

A wormhole joins our imperfect universe with the perfect mirror universe of the Garden of Eden.

Figure Six

Trebla continued, I would like to digress for a moment from the science of this discussion to give you a personal account of how I discovered the reality of the theory of higher dimensions and what it meant to me when I applied it in my own life.

My father was a professor of theoretical physics at a local university in Hungary near where I was raised. He was a militant atheist. My mother was agnostic. I favored my

---

[1] Scientific American, August 2000 The Universes Unseen Dimensions by Nima Arkani-Hamed, Savas Dimopoulos and Georgi Dvali

[2] News article, Daily Republic, April 27,2000

father's position throughout my college and graduate years. When I began to study cosmology I became interested in primitive beliefs about the origin and structure of the universe. I read the mythology of Roman, Greek, Egyptian and other ancient western and oriental civilizations.

Then one time while traveling in the United States, I came across a Gideon Bible in my hotel room. Since I hadn't yet read the Judeo-Christian beliefs about the creation of the universe I began reading about them in Genesis. I was dumbfounded at how compatible they were with modern science. I continued reading the Bible, and then one night as I finished reading the Gospel of John a radiant light encompassed me. Whether the light was actually visible in the room or just in my mind, I do not know. It was as though I had just discovered the secrets of creation.

Jesus was no longer a historical figure, but a living reality who was with me that night. I burst out crying as I remembered what I had read in the fifty third chapter of Isaiah, and what I had just read about His crucifixion and resurrection in the Gospel of John. This was no superstitious legend of Judeo-Christian culture. It had a ring of truth that swept away the bigotry of my past. That night I confessed my sins and pledged my allegiance to the King of Kings, the Lord of my life. That decision has influenced the direction of my entire scientific career and I have been able to confirm many of the miraculous events in the Bible on my subsequent journeys in the Timescape Explorer. You too will be able to see the reality of the past and the manifestation of God's hand in history.

Now let's continue with your orientation. Traditionally, we think of heaven as being above us in space, but logically this can't be, because when we look up at the sky at noon we are looking in exactly the opposite direction than when we look up at the sky at midnight. In both instances we are not looking up in time-space we are looking laterally in three-dimensional space. No matter what direction we look, everything in the present is lateral to us on the time-space plane. Once you leave the gravitational field of earth there is no up or down, everything is lateral to you in time and space.

The Bible tells us heaven is above us, "*Ye men of Galilee, why stand ye gazing up into heaven? this same Jesus, which is taken up from you into heaven, shall so come in like manner as ye have seen him go into heaven.*" **Acts 1:11** But if we were able to look at the sky and see to the outmost reaches of the universe, we would not see heaven, the reason being we would be looking in the wrong direction, because we would be looking laterally in time-space. The Bible is telling you to look up. If you look vertically in time-space (which our physical sensory system is incapable of doing) we would see heaven is closer than the ground we walk on.

There is an analogy that may make this concept clearer. Think of the flat time-space plane of heaven as being a one-way mirror. When we look vertically in time-space we see the reflecting side of the mirror and the images we see are an exact duplication of our own universe, so we are unaware of looking up. On the other hand, God and other heavenly beings are very close, just on the other side of the mirror and they can see everything that's happening on our time-space plane with perfect clarity.

That sounds like a good theory but is there any cosmological evidence to support it. We will find that cosmologists not only seriously entertain the possibility of other universes in higher dimensions, they also believe there are portals of entry to these parallel universes. The Bible tells us there is such a reality. In fact, there may be a number of parallel universes as indicated by the following verse. "*I know a man in Christ who fourteen years ago was caught up to the **third heaven**. Whether it was in the body or out of the body I do not know—God knows.*" **2 Corinthians 12:2** There's a popular myth that there are seven heavens.

Because of the limitation of our five senses we are like a man with the blindfold, unable to see the reality of the universe in which we exist; but we have some indication there's a spiritual dimension to our being we're unable to physically perceive. In other words, I believe mankind is sixth dimensional. More about that later; the observation ports will permit you to see into the fourth dimension, but you'll not be able to describe what you see except theoretically.

Treb continued. There is no argument that we have observable and measurable three dimensional bodies. Earlier in this talk I made a case for fourth and fifth dimensions for physical objects. To restate this we can conceive of a person being seventy-two inches tall, twenty-six inches broad and sixteen inches thick. The person also has a temporal length as part of his physical body. We will assign twenty-five years as his fourth dimensional length. In addition to his physical width he also has a temporal width. Activities are going on in the right side of his body that are entirely different than those going on in the left side of his body. Different things are going on in his head than are going on in his feet. All these activities are lateral to one another in time-space.

Einstein said, and it still holds true, that the only particles of matter currently present in the universe are those particles that were present at the time of the "big bang". Since the time of origin of these particles some have been lost and others have periodically assumed different configurations giving them specific identities: e.g. a star, a planet, a mountain, a tree, a piece of bread, a bowl of soup. All those things are made of subatomic particles such as the electron, proton, neutron, etc., which in turn make up atoms and molecules, and these in turn make up those familiar objects named above.

This is important to understand because we are going back in time to the age of dinosaurs and other prehistoric creatures. As we progress through time back to the present, we will observe the change in configuration of these elementary particles into structures we are familiar with in our everyday life. In other words, some of the elementary particles of your body may be the same ones that were formerly part of a dinosaur or some other prehistoric creature. Furthermore you may have the embarrassing experience of seeing your ancestors in activities about which they would not want you to know.

Since everything each one of you has ever done is still going on in the past, we will spare the feelings of our passengers by not viewing the past eighty years. I realize most of you are hoping to get a glimpse of the future. This will not be possible as we are under strict orders from higher authorities not to enter future 'time-space.'

The speaker system switched to the cockpit. "Treb, this is the Captain speaking, are all your passengers buckled in and ready for take off?"

Trebla pushed a series of buttons. The hatch silently slid closed, red lights on the panel turned to green and the cabin lights dimmed.

"All's Okay back here, Pete, we're ready to fly."

"Good, before we power up I would like to tell your friends a little about the physics of the trip. Are they ready for a short lecture?"

"I think so." She answered, "Go ahead."

Captain Peter Von Rock was a no nonsense astrophysicist engineer, and a pioneer in "time-space" travel. He had done postgraduate research in this field at Cal-Tech, M.I.T., Oxford and Princeton. He was the lead member of the design team that put the project together. The International Space Agency designated the project with the acronym TRUTEST (The Research Unit To Explore Space-Time). There were only two other space engineers qualified to fly the Timescape Explorer.

Captain Von Rock continued. " You'll experience none of the G (Gravitational) forces associated with space travel. That's because our vertical thrust into "time-space" will be 32.769 mm and last only 0.00007 seconds. This will take us just above the galactic membrane that acts as a one-way mirror. That's enough to lift us off our five dimensional "time-space" plane and give us enough "time-space" altitude to skim over the past history of our planet at a height low enough to see things in considerable detail.

"When you are below the galactic membrane trying to look up in "time-space" all you see is the reflection of the flat five dimensional "time-space" plane with which you are familiar. However, when looking down from above the membrane you have a clear view of everything below you, past and present without the limits of the passage of time. The future is already there, but higher authorities have obscured the visual on the "future" port control.

"Treb will explain more about this as we make our journey. One other thing before I turn the mike back to Treb, our speed into the past will range from 1 "space-time" hour per minute to 500,000 "space-time" years per minute. I'm also going to give you a unique experience, and I don't want you to worry about what's happening. This will be perfectly safe and it will give you a graphic demonstration of being involved in what you see. We will stop the passage of time.

"During the demonstration, I'm going to slow the Timescape Explorer to the exact speed toward the past, that time is moving forward on earth. We will prepare you for this state with a short video putting you in a relaxed, blissful mood, a mood you will maintain during the experience. You'll be completely immobilized just as you would be in a photo; frozen in the position you are in at the time we achieve target speed; your heart will not be beating, you will not be breathing and you can't move a muscle. This is not dangerous; once we resume our cruising speed forward or backward all bodily functions return to normal.

Treb will take it from here."

A soft hum filled the cabin, and then Treb's voice came over the speakers "Well folks, we're on our way. In a few moments, I'll open the visual ports so you can see what's going on down below. You're going to see some spectacular events this trip, especially for those of you who know your Bible.

"Until the initiation of hyperdimensional "time-space" exploration, anthropomorphism (attributing human characteristics to God) was frowned upon by most scientists. Now we're ashamed to admit it, but the Bible has understood the existence of hyperdimensional space for thousands of years and we didn't believe it.

"I know it's difficult to conceptualize something you can't visualize as part of your every day life, but what you are about to see may help. First I'm going to open the visual ports only enough for you to see the landscape of the past through a narrow two cm slit. This will give you the impression that activity in the past is occurring exactly as you see it in everyday life. After a few minutes of seeing earthly activity of the past occurring as you are accustomed to seeing it I'm going to open the ports all the way. When this happens you will see nothing is moving. People, animal and machines will be seen as the five dimensional linear time-space objects they are. The illusion of motion is created by a change in the relationship of different segments of objects to one another.

I'll stop talking for a while and give you a chance to concentrate on the scenery."

Trebla took her seat next to a port and looked at the landscape unfolding below her. On her face, was a happy smile like a child showing off a new toy.

The scene observed through the narrow slit looked exactly like that depicted in the movie *Jurassic Park*. Prehistoric animals wandered across the lush primitive landscape. Huge, weird looking creatures flew across the sky. It was similar to a trip through an exhibit at the Epcot Center. Finally Trebla stretched, got to her feet and picked up the microphone. "It's time to see what the past is really like. I'm going to open the visual port all the way and give you a broad view of the 'time-space' plane."

The shutter across the ports slowly slid open. There was a gasp by the passengers as they tried to grasp the significance of what they were seeing. There was no way of describing the shape of the objects in the scene below them.

The creatures they had perceived to be moving a few moments ago were motionless. Their shape was different. They were seen in their five dimensional temporal length; from birth to death, including their ancestors and progeny. The entire "time-space" plane appeared to be a model with features and creatures made of modeling clay. It was like looking at a moving picture running either forward or backward with any frame or segment being brought into focus at will. The sequence of frames gave the appearance of motion, but in totality there was no motion at all.

Elizabeth Spencer's hand shot up. Liz was a fourteen-year-old high school student chosen for the trip by high school teachers belonging to the International Association for Science Knowledge (Acronym: I ASK). She was a beautiful girl with a quick facile mind. Her budding maturity of body and intellect gave promise of an exceptional future.

"Yes, Liz, do you have a question?" Treb asked.

"Well, to me this indicates evolution didn't occur. If nothing moves there can be no change. God must have created the entire universe, past, present and future all at once. In order to have evolutionary development there has to be motion of some sort before you can have change. All these creatures are merging into their successors as a static entity. From what we are seeing of the past, everything has been here motionless from the beginning, and I would expect that to be true of the future."

"That's a very astute observation," Treb replied. "Until very recently science has accepted the theories of Newton and Einstein, but early in the year 2000 **Julian Barbour** challenged the concept of motion in his book entitled, *The End of Time: The Next Revolution In Physics.* From our observation, it appears Dr. Barbour is right. Motion of physical objects is an illusion created by the passage of time. Paradoxically Einstein said, "People like us, who believe in physics, know that the distinction between past, present and future is only a stubbornly persistent illusion."[3]

"Now I'm going to restore the visual port to the narrow slit again because the drama of what you are about to see is much more exciting if you see it happen with the illusion of motion. It's the difference between seeing the pictures of a football game by holding up a strip of movie film of a game to the light and projecting that same film in motion on the screen." Treb continued as the shutters on the ports slid closed to a narrow slit. "Now look toward the horizon. There you will see a spot of light moving toward you. The time is about 60 million years ago according to our time frame."

The spot of light grew larger and larger. Time-space Explorer moved to a higher altitude. The size of objects on

---

[3] Hyperspace p.232

earth shrunk to a point where they were barely visible. The geographical boundaries of what would eventually be the East Coast of the United States became clearly discernable.

The ball of fire approaching the earth was huge. It was a meteor, and we watched in fascination as it slammed into the Gulf of Mexico. Steam and smoke billowed skyward. Captain von Rock moved us high above the chaotic catastrophe that was occurring on earth. A thick cloud of smoke steam and debris drifted around the world.

"Well" I said, "That's the end of the dinosaurs."

"Afraid not," said Treb, "Look out your port."

The shutter was still closed to a slit, but Captain Pete had reversed our course and when I looked, all the creatures were going backward just like a movie film in reverse. Then Treb opened the ports all the way. The meteor we had seen streaking toward the earth was no longer a ball of metal rock and gas, but a stationary cylinder projecting back into the distant reaches of the galaxy. The earth had resumed the appearance of a vast molded clay model of prehistoric animals and vegetation.

"Now Captain Pete is going to bring us up to the age of mankind. We will be traveling about 500,000 years a minute so it will take almost fifteen minutes to reach our destination of about 50,000 years prior to the time you started this trip. At that speed, you will not be able to distinguish much of the landscape so I suggest you put your seats in the reclining position, relax and take a little snooze. The ports will be at slit aperture so if you want to you can look out. I will be back on the air when we near our destination. In spite of the speed and distance we were traveling, there was no sensation of motion. Inside the Timescape Explorer it seemed we were standing perfectly still and the earth was spinning at fantastic speed in the opposite direction from it's usual rotation.

Chapter Six
Earth Worms And Worm Holes

Wormholes have been described in theoretical physics as portals for time travel into the past, or as shortcuts to different parts of our universe; however, they may also be considered as connections to parallel universes.[1]

Two parallel planes superimposed on one another may graphically represent parallel universes. Normally two such planes never interact with each other. However, at times, wormholes or tubes may open up between them making communication and travel between them possible. This is now a subject of intense interest among theoretical physicists.[2]

✦   ✦   ✦   ✦   ✦

Dr. Treb Nietsnie offered coffee, soda and snacks to her passengers and then picked up the microphone.

"Dr. Reynolds, one of our passengers, is a Bible scholar and because many of the sights we are going to see in the next segment of our trip are related to Biblical events, I've asked him to narrate this portion of our journey. We're temporarily closing the ports until we arrive on station"

Dr. Bill Reynolds was a physician, not a theologian, but he made a hobby of studying the relationship of higher dimensions to theology. He had a mischievous twinkle in his eye and was brimming with enthusiasm to tell the rest of us his views on what we were about to see.

He took the mike from Trebla and said, "Hello, fellow earthworms. You know from God's perspective that's exactly what we are, and from a hyperdimensional viewpoint

[1] Hyperspace p. P.24

[2] Hyperspace p. 19

that is what we look like. In fact, God said, *"Behold even to the moon, and it shineth not; yea, the stars are not pure in his sight.* ***How much less man, that is a worm? and the son of man, which is a worm?"*** *Job 25:5 and 6*

"Do not be afraid, O **worm** *Jacob, and ye men of Israel."* ***Isaiah 41:13-14*** I'm sure almost everyone takes the designation of "worm" as a figure of speech; interestingly enough it can be taken literally, because in the eyes of God our physical bodies can be seen as worms, *earth*worms. We have seen that our physical bodies have a longitudinal time dimension, from past to future that we are unable to visually perceive. But if we can picture, in the abstract, our three dimensional body extending through time, from birth to death, in their fourth dimensional configuration, you can better understand it's worm-like appearance. You should also remember that the Christian earthworm will be changed to a new creature in eternity; like a caterpillar turns into a butterfly. "Who, will transform our lowly bodies so they will be like His glorious body." ***Philippians 3:21***

Dr. Fred Allan Wolf, a theoretical physicist from UCLA, puts it this way, "Your whole life history lies like a giant centipede stuck in plastic, with one end tiny and baby-like in form and the other end old and decrepit. All your ups and downs are just wiggles in the **worm**."[3]

Bill Reynolds continued. "One of my pre-med courses in college was embryology. It was in this course I had one of the most difficult assignments I was ever given. My professor gave me a box of slides on which cross sections of a salamander had been mounted. The specimen was sliced into cross sections, from one end to the other like a loaf of bread, mounted on microscope slides and stained with a dye that helped to differentiate the various internal structures. My assignment was to look at these multiple cross sections and draw a sagittal (longitudinal) view showing what the internal structures would look like if the salamander had been sliced down the middle and divided equally into a right and left side.

[3] Parallel Universes p.120

"That is similar to what I'm asking you to do. Each moment of your life is seen as a three dimensional cross section of your time-space long body. I'm asking you to look at the entire series of cross section images of that body and visualize them as a longitudinal time-space object. It's difficult to conceptualize, but that's what you have just done with the dinosaurs.

"If you took a movie film of your entire life, cut out your picture from each individual frame, starting with the first image as a baby and stacked each succeeding picture of yourself on top of the next one, the pile would represent a longitudinal view of your four dimensional long time-space body, as depicted by the combination of three dimensional cross sections of your fourth dimensional self. However remember each cross section will be three not two dimensional.

"The people you will see in this segment of our trip will appear in their three dimensional configuration, the same as if you were watching a 3-D movie. Their lives will be time compressed into a few minutes in order for us to stay within the time frame of our trip."

Treb interrupted Bill's talk. "We're on station; it's time to open the ports."

"Good," Bill responded, "By special concession from higher authorities, we have been granted permission for you to have a special treat. Instead of looking down this time, I want you to look up."

The ports opened. A gasp of amazement rose from the passengers. Hovering just above them, slightly above eye level was the most beautiful garden they had ever seen. It seemed to be floating in space. The trees were tall and perfectly formed. Shrubs and flowers were in full bloom; their shape, size and color was dazzling. Perfectly kept paths and lawns gave evidence of loving care. Orchards of picture perfect fruits and nuts appeared ready to harvest, and streams, waterfalls and lakes were scattered with abandon throughout.

"I've seen the great gardens of the world." Bill said. "I've traveled in the tropics where there was a profusion of gorgeous flowers and vegetation, but nothing I've seen on earth can begin to compare with the incomprehensible beauty lying before us."

Near the center of the garden was a huge artesian well spouting enormous geysers of crystal clear water hundreds of feet into the air. The water falling to the ground collected into a broad stream that fed a lake, and from this lake flowed four rivers.

On the banks of the stream coming from the well, was a meticulously kept park. In the center of the park were two trees bearing the most beautiful, luscious fruit of which one could conceive. Those tending the park would stop and admire the trees, but no one touched them. The people working in the garden were singing and laughing as they went about their chores.

Bill Reynolds was smiling as he resumed his commentary. "By now," he said, "you realize you're looking at the Garden of Eden. But I'm sure some of you have questions about the reality lying before you. Before I answer them, I want you to see your first wormhole."

As they continued looking, the shadow of a depression appeared in the ground near the two beautiful trees in the center of the Garden. A man and a woman, who were standing on the ground where the shadow appeared, were talking to someone we couldn't see. Unlike the others, we had seen they were very distressed. Suddenly they disappeared and in their place stood figures with wings, clothed in dazzling white robes and holding swords flashing fire from the brilliant light surrounding them.

"Now look down." Bill said.

They looked down where the depression in the ground had appeared, and saw our world: a wild, tangled jungle with the two people standing waist deep in weeds and brambles. They were not alone; primitive, large brained bipedal primates, clothed in animal skins and using crude tools could be seen in the distance.

Adam and Eve immediately recognized their predicament. They were highly intelligent and possessed remarkable skills, so they set out to build a shelter and forage for food.

A hand was hesitantly raised. It was Al Watts, an electrical engineer from Forestville. "What I see doesn't coincide with what my minister teaches in his Bible class."

Dr. Reynolds smiled, "I'm not surprised; I haven't heard anyone describe this scene either, so let's see what the Bible says." He was holding a well worn Bible. He opened it to **Genesis 1** and read verses **27 and 28**,

"*So God created man in his own image, in the image of God he created him; male and female he created them. God blessed them and said to them, "Be fruitful and increase in number; fill the earth and subdue it. Rule over the fish of the sea and the birds of the air and over every living creature that moves on the ground. So God created man in his own image, in the image of God created he him; male and female created he them."* **Genesis 1:27-28**

He then proceeded to read, "*So he drove out the man; and he placed at the east of the garden of Eden Cherubims, and a flaming sword which turned every way, to keep the way of the tree of life."* **Genesis 3: 24**

"I think there are many misconceptions about the creation story," Bill continued, "many of which are not consistent with our knowledge of science or the Bible. If we examine the Scriptures carefully and compare it to the accepted theories of modern day science, we'll find a remarkable correlation between the two.

This is already outlined in your information packet but because this is such an important aspect of our Christian Faith, I would like to take a few minutes to explain my views on creation, and the fall of man that you have just seen.

I think of our universe as a flat five dimensional tapestry. It has a beginning, "*In the beginning God created the heaven and the earth."* **Genesis 1:1** and it has an end. (*That day will bring about the destruction of the heavens by fire, and the elements will melt in the heat:* **2 Peter 3:12**). "*And sware by him that liveth for ever and ever, who created* *heaven, and the things that therein are, and the earth, and the things that therein are, and the sea, and the things which are therein, **that there should be time no longer**."* **Revelation 10:6**

Dr. Reynolds continued. When time ends (the terminal margin of the time-space tapestry) space ends. You can't have space without time. To travel beyond the point where time stops would require more time, and if there is no more time, there is no more space.

According to the cosmologists, and their concept of time, the universe came into being about fifteen billion years ago. But according to the Bible, the way I understand it, the actual age of the universe is moot. The reason I say this is that I have a paradigm of creation different from any I've heard from either the scientists or the theologians. My reasoning is simple, Biblical, logical and based on the following assumptions.

One of the things we know about God is that He exists outside the limits of time and space. He's a hyperdimensional being to whom there is no past, present or future; all things exist in an eternal present. In other words, God sees the time-space plane of our universe from its very beginning to its very end, as "NOW".

In the literature you received prior to this trip, the position was established that 'time' as we conceive it is an illusion. Einstein said so; physicists accept it and the Bible confirms the scientific view of time. "God said to Moses, *"I AM WHO I AM. This is what you are to say to the Israelites. 'I AM has sent me to you.'"* **Exodus 3:14** He wasn't the God of history, or the God of the future; He is the God of the eternal present (Now), past, present and future, all of which exist simultaneously with God. It is written, *"I am the Alpha and the Omega," says the Lord God, "who is, and who was, and who is to come, the Almighty."* **Revelation 1:8** *"I am Alpha and Omega the beginning and the end."* **Revelation 1:8, 21:6, 22:13** *"This is what the LORD says— Israel's King and Redeemer, the LORD Almighty: I am the first and I am the last; apart from me there is no God."* **Isaiah 44:6**

If time is non-existent with God then what He created He created instantaneously, not in seven days, or in fifteen billion years. Time is finite; it's nothing more than a measurement across a static five dimensional plane, one edge of which is the "Big Bang," the other end being the Day of the Lord, as mentioned in *2 Peter 3:10*.

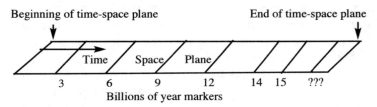

Beginning of time-space plane   End of time-space plane

Time / Space / Plane /

3   6   9   12   14   15   ???

Billions of year markers

Starting at the beginning edge of this time-space plane, and running to its final margin, are markers of linear space–time that we have labeled as days, years, centuries, millennia, etc. These markers are not being set up day-by-day, or year-by-year; they are merely marking the position on the time-space plain of events that have already happened; and to God they are all visible as an eternal present.

All that ever occurred in the past is still occurring now. All that will occur in the future is already present on the time-space plane. For the Christian liberated from the bondage of Time a certain degree of choice has been restored.

Figure Seven

In my opinion, both the old earth evolutionists and the young earth creationists are wrong. The past geologic ages, including the present one in which we live, were laid down in six layers. Each layer was created from its first appearance to its disappearance at the end of time. The entire life span of that period of creation from beginning to end was laid down before the next layer was started. (The crustaceans of the pre-Cambrian age went through their life cycles, became fossils and turned into hydrocarbons before the next layer of creation was started. As each layer was placed upon the other there was a blending of elements giving geologic continuity to the final product.

The original word for "day" used in these passages can also be interpreted as periods of time. I believe the original word used to define the beginning and the end of the creation process for the segment of creation just completed refers to a period of time not a twenty-four hour day. If you want to be literal about the evening and the morning being a similar period to our present perception of time, remember the black box at the Griffith Planetarium. Evening and morning are not determined by the motion of celestial bodies, or watches or clocks, but by the change of the relationship of celestial bodies. The celestial bodies are not moving, only the passage of time is moving. God made time periods from tubular bodies of light after His creation, not before, and that's what my Bible says:

*And God said, "Let there be light," and there was light. God saw that the light was good, and he separated the light from the darkness. God called the light "day," and the darkness he called "night." And there was evening, and there was morning—the first day. So God made the expanse and separated the water under the expanse from the water above it. And it was so. God called the expanse "sky." And there was evening, and there was morning—the second day." **Genesis 1: 3-4,5,8**

I interpret this to say there was no first day until God finished His creation for that particular period, the same for the second, third, fourth, fifth and sixth day and He hasn't declared a morning and an evening for the seventh day so that period is still open ended." **Genesis 1: 3,4,5** and **8** *"By the seventh day God had finished the work he had been doing; (There has been no new creation since the creation of mankind on the sixth segment of creation) so on the seventh day he rested from all his work. And God blessed the seventh day and made it holy, because on it he rested from all the work of creating that he had done. This is the account of the heavens and the earth when they were created." **Genesis 2:2-4**

We really don't know when God started the slit in the time curtain moving, or whether it has always moved at a constant speed. There is presumptive evidence that our concept of time did not begin until Adam and Eve sinned.

St. Augustine believed this to be true. The presumptive logic is based on **Romans 5:12** *"Therefore, just as sin entered the world through one man, and death through sin, and in this way death came to all men, because all sinned."* The passage of time is the sentence of death, so it can be assumed that before sin entered into the equation death was not inevitable.

There's good reason to believe Adam and Eve lived for a very long time in the Garden of Eden before they sinned and death became inevitable. Some Biblical numerologists have concluded they lived thirty-five hundred years before the fall. We have no way of knowing for sure, because before they sinned time was an entirely different phenomenon. It could have been a few years, or many thousands. It had to be a span of several years at least, because Eve had born children before the fall. *"To the woman he said, "I will greatly increase your pains in childbearing; with pain you will give birth to children."* **Genesis 3:16**

The question at once arises as to what happened to her children born before the *fall*. I think she had many children, none of which were tainted by their parent's sin. Although Bible scholars have other interpretations for the verses I'm going to use to support my position, I think my interpretation is more plausible.

"The sons of God saw that the daughters of men were beautiful, and they married any of them they chose. There were giants in the earth in those days; and also after that, when the sons of God came in unto the daughters of men, and they bare children to them, the same became mighty men which were of old, men of renown." **Genesis 6:2 and 6:4**

Adam and his progeny are consistently referred to in the Bible as 'sons of God'. I interpret this passage to indicate that Adam's unfallen sons came down to earth through a wormhole and married into the sinful families that were established by Adam and Eve after their fall. (This raises some serious problems. Admittedly, I'm on shaky ground in some of my assumptions, but if I can get you to study your Bible and other orthodox resources, my novel opinions will have been productive.) Genetically, they had to be human to have children by another human. Even slight differences in genetic makeup make fertile cross mating impossible. It's easy to understand how undefiled sons of God would contribute superior genes to the fertilization of sinful women resulting in "men of great renown"; however, these "men of great renown" are contaminated by the original sin of Eve through their mother and their children would have the potential for extreme sinful excesses as well as for their great deeds. A question arises as to whether these sons of God were sinning by having sex with post-fall women. I don't think so. As pre-fall children of Adam they were created to have sex. The post-fall daughters of Adam were ligitimate mates.

The next reference is, *"Now there was a day when the sons of God came to present themselves before the LORD," Job 1:6* Who were these sons of God if they were not progeny of Adam and Eve before the fall? The Bible clearly allows a distinction between angels and 'sons of God'. *"When the morning stars sang together, and all the sons of God shouted for joy?" Job 38:7* In this instance 'the sons of God' are plural and the verse implies a large number of them, so it does not refer to Jesus.

It may be stretching a parable a little but the following fits the situation perfectly.

*"Suppose one of you has a hundred sheep and loses one of them. Does he not leave the ninety-nine in the open country and go after the lost sheep until he finds it? And when he finds it, he joyfully puts it on his shoulders and goes home. Then he calls his friends and neighbors together and says, 'Rejoice with me; I have found my lost sheep. I tell you that in the same way there will **be more rejoicing in heaven over one sinner who repents than over ninety-nine righteous persons who do not need to repent." Luke 15:4-7***

Jesus left the ninety-nine sheep in heaven and came to earth to save the lost sheep. There was more rejoicing in heaven over the one sinner who repented than over the ninety-nine who didn't need to repent. The ninety-nine could not apply to humans on earth, because we know from other scriptures that *"All have sinned and come short of the glory of God.*" **Romans 3:23**; and need to repent of their sins, while the ninety and nine who do not need to repent are already in the fold.

Then one of the elders asked me, "*These in white robes—* "*who are they, and where did they come from?*" **Revelation 7:13** Who were they? They weren't the apostles. Couldn't they be the priesthood of our unfallen brothers in heaven? Also there is another unexplained person in the Scriptures, "*You are a priest forever, in the order of Melchizedek.*" — — He (Jesus) became the source of eternal salvation for all who obey him, and was designated by God to be high priest in the order of Melchizedek. **Hebrews 5:10** I have heard preachers say that Melchizedek referred to Christ, (see **Genesis 14: 18**) but that doesn't make sense, because the person referred to, which seems to be Jesus, is to be the source of salvation and a priest **after the order of Melchizedek**. I'm aware that this is not conventional theology, but I'm unaware of any substantial Scriptural evidence that refutes these assumptions.

Well, let's take a quick look at some of the other wormholes. We don't have time to view all of them, but we are going to see a few of them.

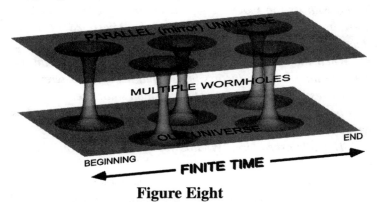

Figure Eight

"*But the LORD came down* (through a worm hole) *to see the city and the tower that the men were building.* **Genesis 11:5** *Abraham looked up and saw three men standing nearby. When he saw them, he hurried from the entrance of his tent to meet them and bowed low to the ground. He said, "If I have found favor in your eyes, my lord, do not pass your servant by. Let a* *little water be brought, and then you may all wash your feet and rest under this tree. Let me get you something to eat, so you can be refreshed and then go on your way—now that you have come to your servant."*

"Very well," they answered, "do as you say."

So Abraham hurried into the tent to Sarah. "Quick," he said, "get three seahs of fine flour and knead it and bake some bread."

Then he ran to the herd and selected a choice, tender calf and gave it to a servant, who hurried to prepare it. He then brought some curds and milk and the calf that had been prepared, and set these before them. While they ate, he stood near them under a tree." **Genesis 18: 2-8**

Here we have the Lord coming down to earth and an angel coming down to visit and also three men that came from some extraterrestrial location. The men were humans; they wore ordinary clothes, ate earthly food and drank beverages, but they were not citizens of this world. They came through a wormhole, or time warp. Remember, we are not talking about spirits or visions, but substantive people.

"He had a dream in which he saw a stairway resting on the earth, with its top reaching to heaven, and the angels of God were ascending and descending on it." **Genesis 28:12** *— So Jacob was left alone, and a man wrestled with him till daybreak.*

When the man saw that he could not overpower him, he touched the socket of Jacob's hip so that his hip was wrenched as he wrestled with the man. Then the man said, "Let me go, for it is daybreak." But Jacob replied, "I will not let you go unless you bless me."

The man asked him, "What is your name?" "Jacob," he answered.

Then the man said, "Your name will no longer be Jacob, but Israel, because you have struggled with God and with men and have overcome."

Jacob said, "Please tell me your name." But he replied, "Why do you ask my name?" Then he blessed him there. **Genesis 32:25–29** This sounds as if Jacob wrestled with a human, not an angel.

"When the servant of the man of God got up and went out early the next morning, an army with horses and chariots had

surrounded the city. "Oh, my lord, what shall we do?" the servant asked.

"Don't be afraid," the prophet answered. "Those who are with us are more than those who are with them." And Elisha prayed, "O LORD, open his eyes so he may see." Then the LORD opened the servant's eyes, and he looked and saw the hills full of horses and chariots of fire all around Elisha. **2 Kings 6:15** I believe these were real heavenly troops from a parallel universe.

"Enoch walked with God; then he was no more, because God took him away." **Genesis 5:24** (Through a worm hole.)

"Then King Nebuchadnezzar leaped to his feet in amazement and asked his advisers, "Weren't there three men that we tied up and threw into the fire?" They replied, "Certainly, O king."

He said, "Look! I see four men walking around in the fire, unbound and unharmed, and the fourth looks like a son of the gods." **Daniel 3:24-25**

The appearance of these people, and the many other examples of extraterrestrial visitors, are physical entities with human characteristics, eating, drinking and wearing appropriate clothing. They had to come from a physical location, and we know that was not from distant galaxy. They appear suddenly and disappear suddenly, yet they are substantive. Where do they come from and where do they go?

There is only one logical answer; they are visitors from an extra-terrestrial universe that is very close (One scientific paper says a parallel universe may be only one millimeter away.)

"Do not forget to entertain strangers, for by so doing some people have entertained angels without knowing it." **Hebrews 13:2** There are extra-terrestrial beings in the world today (both good and bad.). They look like people, they talk like people, they dress like people and eat and drink like people. Some may be our distant brothers by our common parents Adam and Eve. Whoever they are, time warps and worm holes are real and of theological significance.

Inter-universe travel by extra-terrestrials is not a rare occurrence, as you can see from the Biblical accounts that have just been cited. The dream of Jacob's ladder is symbolic, with elements of truth that are hard for us to perceive. **Genesis 28:12 and 13**

"*Therefore, since we are surrounded by such a great cloud of witnesses, let us throw off everything that hinders and the sin that so easily entangles, and let us run with perseverance the race marked out for us.*" **Hebrews 12:1**

Those witnesses are real people, and just because we don't hear or see them doesn't mean they're not physically there, any more than a man who is blind and deaf, attending a concert can deny that there is an orchestra playing a Beethoven symphony."

Bill Reynolds took a sip of hot coffee.

"We're going to do fly-bys of some of these worm holes. Captain Pete will explore which of the past wormholes are still open and active. Most of them have been closed, but we may find a few that aren't. I can assure you there are numerous ones in our future, but they're off limits to us on this trip. Keep your eyes and port screens wide open, we can't linger in the area of an open wormhole. If we see one we will pass it at high speed, and you'll miss it if you're not watching closely."

An air of excitement filled the cabin as wormhole after wormhole flew past the ports. What was seen can't be described, but the profound effect on the passengers gave evidence that their lives would never be the same again.

Treb picked up her microphone; "Well friends, the fly-bys end our voyage. It's been a pleasure to have you as our guests, and I think you will find your life will be enriched by this experience. Thank you for being with us."

There was a slight jolt as Timescape Explorer penetrated the galactic membrane of our universe and reentered the Time-Space Terminal. The cabin lights grew brighter and the hatch of the Timescape Explorer silently slid open.

Bill Reynolds looked at the clock in the terminal. The second hand on the clock had advanced exactly eighty-seven seconds since the hatch had slid closed and the sleek vehicle had taken him thousands of light years into the past and back again. He said to himself, "Time really is an illusion."

*(Note) For those of you who havent noticed, the name Trebla Nietsnie is Albert Einstein spelled backwards.

Chapter Seven
Seeing The Invisible

A young moon cast its pale beams across the rippling black water and soft puffs of fog drifted across the seascape. There was a foreboding, empty silence to the night that smothered the invisible drama of terror playing itself out in the briny depths below. Underneath the restless surface of the sea a United States Navy submarine was in deep trouble, —and I was there.

Water was pouring down the conning tower hatch; the noise from the pumps was deafening; a stream of oil from the overhead made the deck as slippery as an ice rink, and the sub was heeling over on its starboard side. If the list became much greater we would lose the air in the starboard trim tank, capsize and lie helplessly on the bottom. What started out as a marvelous adventure was rapidly turning into a horrible nightmare.

I was the medical officer at the Narragansett Naval Torpedo Station in Narragansett Bay, Rhode Island. It was September 1943 and World War II was in full swing. I'd never been on a submarine before and I thought it would be a great experience to take a ride on one. Subs regularly came into the torpedo station for servicing, and to go out on the torpedo range to practice firing torpedoes with dummy warheads.

It was a brisk fall morning when the captain of one of the subs came into the clinic for a minor medical problem. While I was taking care of his medical needs I said, "Commander, is there any chance of my bumming a ride when you go out on the practice range to fire your torpedoes?"

"Sure," he answered, "we'll be going out about 1700 hours this evening and you're welcome to come along."

When I reported to the dock, at the appointed time, I noticed things were not going well. It was a very old submarine and the crew had been trying to load their dummy torpedoes since 1500 hours (3:00 P.M.). One of the torpedoes had gotten stuck in the hatch and they were having a terrible time trying to get it loose. It was two hours later before the torpedoes were loaded and we cast off.

As we approached the torpedo range the skipper picked up his "mike" and said, "Prepare to dive."

The Chief Petty Officer pulled out a little book with a checklist in it. Carefully he checked the condition of components listed for safe submergence. Hatches, valves and gauges were examined to make sure of the watertight integrity of the vessel and its ability to function properly under water.

"All Okay Captain, vessel ready to submerge," he called out as he completed his inspection and put his little book back in his pocket.

The Captain activated his "mike". He acknowledged the report and gave the order to submerge. "Let's do it, — dive; down 10 degrees"

A bustle of activity occurred as the crew went about their respective tasks. The plainsmen responded to the order, and we slid silently beneath the waves. Within a few minutes we were on the torpedo practice range.

Again the Captain spoke into the "mike". "Prepare bow torpedoes one and two for launch."

The torpedo tubes flooded, lights on the control panels flashed and changed colors. The Executive Officer watched as the arrows on dials shifted to their torpedo-firing mode.

"We're ready to launch the bow torpedoes, Skipper." He said to the captain.

"Up periscope —- fire one," the captain said.

No sooner had the torpedo left the tube than the second command came, "Fire two".

With the firing of the two torpedoes the bow lightened and there was a noticeable change in the angle of the vessel. We were practically sitting on the bottom of Narragansett

Bay and when the bow lightened, the Captain, afraid the sub's propellers would foul in the mud, barked, "Blow the trim tanks."

In the noise and confusion associated with the firing of the torpedoes the crewman on the starboard side heard the order, but the crewman on the port side didn't. Consequently the increasing buoyancy from the trim tank on the starboard side was pushing the sub into a dangerous list to the port.

The Captain screamed an order to stop the compressors that were filling the starboard trim tank with air. The noise of the compressor was so loud the crewman didn't hear him. Slowly we were capsizing. Water poured from the conning tower haich. The Executive Officer tried to catch a stream of oil that was coming from the overhead, in a coffee cup without success. The deck was not only tilted to a dangerous angle but it was becoming too slippery from the oil to walk on safely.

The Captain raced across the deck and pounded on the back of the crewman blowing the port trim tank. "Shut it down!" He screamed. The compressor stopped and a deadly silence ensued. The Exec made his way to the trim tank controls and flooded the starboard tank until the sub regained its trim.

Much to my relief I found out that the water pouring from the conning tower hatch into the control room was from the bilges in the conning tower and the watertight integrity of the sub had not been breached.

The Exec poured me a cup of coffee and one for himself.

"I've been in subs for two years," he said, "I've never dived like that before and I hope I never have to dive like that again. The problem is," he continued, "we have a green crew who have never handled a dive alone before. Our regular crew is on shore leave and the Captain thought it would be a good opportunity to break the newcomers in to the responsibility of a dive."

"Well," I said, "I won't forget this experience for a long, long time."

"Neither will I," said the Exec.

I sat sipping my coffee, thanking God for saving us from what could have been a catastrophe.

A short time later the Exec said to me, "We've surfaced. If you would like to, you can go up on the sail deck."

Eagerly I climbed the ladder to the outside world. The cool night breeze washed the lingering fear of this frightening experience from my mind. The moon was low on the horizon and pillows of mist still floated across the water. The black nose of the sub pushed huge ripples in front of it and all was silent.

As I looked around, I realized the terror of what had just happened was invisible from the surface of the bay. The physical reality of what was going on beneath the waves was totally undetectable to those who might be floating above us.

The world in which we live is much like that. Beneath the surface of our lives, and the lives of others, dangerous and even catastrophic events may occur without anyone else knowing it. Furthermore, there is a world of reality below the surface of our sensory perception that's very real.

In previous chapters, we have discussed the tangible reality of persons and events in hyperdimensional realms, but we must not neglect the fact that evil forces and persons are just as substantial as are the good ones. Satan, when he tempted Eve was a material entity. In Job, Satan was just as much a material reality as he was in the Garden of Eden.

"The LORD said to Satan, "Where have you come from?" Satan answered the LORD, "From roaming through the earth and going back and forth in it." ***Job 1:7*** (Could this not be an actual physical presence expressed in the form of an individual similar to the messengers from God who appeared to Abraham, et al, and is he not still roaming the earth looking for victims?)

It's important for Christians to realize we are not just confronting vague, nebulous spirits of evil, but entities just as real as the three men that appeared to Abraham.

*"Abraham looked up and saw three men standing nearby,
—Let me get you something to eat, so you can be refreshed
and then go on your way."*

"Very well," they answered, "do as you say." **Genesis 18:2-5**

Many people consider evil as bad thoughts and selfish
acts. But evil is much more than that; it's also a physical
force in a hyperdimensional world of evil beings, some of
whom eat food, and wear clothes just like the rest of us, and
are bent on persuading us to disobey God and to succumb to
evil desires like those that caused Adam and Eve to sin.
There is more reality than most people imagine, in **C.S.
Lewis'** *Screw Tape Letters* a senior demon instructs a novice
demon how to tempt people.

Prepare yourselves with much prayer before going with
me on a voyage into the evil world of psychic phenomena.
With a clear understanding of what is going on one can
more easily differentiate the good, the bad and the indifferent.

There's a lot of confusion about the realm of the supernatural. It's not the phenomenon that's evil; it's the influence
it has on peoples lives and how the power it possesses is
used. Let us keep in mind that all power is given to Jesus.
*"Jesus came and spake unto them, saying, All power is given
unto me in heaven and in earth."* **Matthew 28:18** He didn't
say *some power*; He said *all* power.

Satan has no power of his own; his only power is misap-
propriated power from God, and that is what makes it so
dangerous; it's God's power used inappropriately. God has
given us the ability to use the supernatural power of fixed
spiritual laws to accomplish specific things for Him. Satan
tries to convince us these abilities are our just inheritance
and we can use them as we please for our own selfish interests. Using them for good brings blessings and fulfillment
of God's plan; using them for selfish reasons can bring unhappiness and disaster.

The linemen for public utility companies work with
transmission lines that sometimes carry thousands of volts
of electricity. Without the proper knowledge and equipment

for their protection they could be fried to a crisp. We're going to examine the knowledge and equipment God has given us to meet the dangers and spiritual challenges of the psychic world that surrounds us. We're going to discuss psychic phenomena that are poorly understood and may be the source of either drawing us closer to God, or alienating us from Him. Only by the power given us by God, through the blood of Jesus Christ, can we deal with the forces of evil.

"The weapons we fight with are not the weapons of the world. On the contrary, they have divine power to demolish strongholds." **2 Corinthians 10:4** *"Finally, be strong in the Lord and in his mighty power. Put on the full armor of God so that you can take your stand against the devil's schemes. For our struggle is not against flesh and blood, but against the rulers, against the authorities, against the powers of this dark world and against the spiritual forces of evil in the heavenly (Hyperdimensional) realms. Therefore put on the full armor of God, so that when the day of evil comes, you may be able to stand your ground, and after you have done everything, to stand. Stand firm then, with the belt of truth buckled around your waist, with the breastplate of right-eousness in place, and with your feet fitted with the readiness that comes from the gospel of peace. In addition to all this, take up the shield of faith, with which you can ex-tinguish all the flaming arrows of the evil one. Take the helmet of salvation and the sword of the Spirit, which is the word of God, and pray in the Spirit on all occasions with all kinds of prayers and requests. With this in mind, be alert."* **Ephesians 6:10-18**

We must fight evil with all our strength, but we must also remember there are times when the foe is greater than we can cope with, and that the battle must be turned completely over to the LORD.

"The LORD said to Satan, 'The LORD rebuke you, Satan! The LORD, who has chosen Jerusalem, rebuke you!' **Zechariah 3:2** *But even the archangel Michael, when he was disputing with the devil about the body of Moses, did*

not dare to bring a slanderous accusation against him, but said, 'The Lord rebuke you!'" **Jude 1:9**

At times, we may be dealing with forces far beyond our normal spiritual capabilities to handle. We must be sure we are fully clothed and armed for this battle and that we remain under the direct command and protection of the Captain of our salvation.

All psychic phenomena are natural, and operate in accordance with divine laws established by God from before the beginning of time. Because of the sin of Adam and Eve, and our own predilection to sin, God chose to limit our ability to use certain psychic powers, except in special circumstances and under His direction, because our hearts are evil. *"The heart is deceitful above all things and beyond cure. Who can understand it?"* **Jeremiah 17:9** He wants to protect us from using those powers for sinful, selfish and destructive purposes. Remember, the forces of evil are not only spirits; some have substantive bodies and tangibly exist, both on earth and in hyperdimensional space.

The Bible is perfectly clear about meddling with psychic phenomena.

"Let no one be found among you who sacrifices his son or daughter in the fire, who practices divination or sorcery, interprets omens, engages in witchcraft or casts spells, or who is a medium or spiritist or who consults the dead. Anyone who does these things is detestable to the LORD. **Deuteronomy 18:12** *"Manasseh — did evil in the eyes of the LORD he bowed down to all the starry hosts and worshiped them. He sacrificed his sons in the fire in the Valley of Ben Hinnom, practiced sorcery, divination and witchcraft, and consulted mediums and spiritists. He did much evil in the eyes of the LORD, — he observed times, and used enchantments, and used witchcraft, and dealt with a familiar spirit, and with wizards: he wrought much evil in the sight of the LORD, to provoke him to anger."* **2 Chronicles 33:1-6**

The story of Saul consulting the medium of Endor indicates a physical confrontation between Saul and Samuel. I think there is credible evidence there was a substantive element to this encounter. The event is recorded in *1 Samuel* chapter *28*.

"Saul then said to his attendants, "Find me a woman who is a medium, so I may go and inquire of her. "There is one in Endor," they said.

So Saul disguised himself, putting on other clothes, and at night he and two men went to the woman. "Consult a spirit for me," he said, "and bring up for me the one I name."

But the woman said to him, "Surely you know what Saul has done. He has cut off the mediums and spiritists from the land. Why have you set a trap for my life to bring about my death?"

Saul swore to her by the LORD, "As surely as the LORD lives, you will not be punished for this."

Then the woman asked, "Whom shall I bring up for you?"

"Bring up Samuel," he said.

When the woman saw Samuel, she cried out at the top of her voice and said to Saul, "Why have you deceived me? You are Saul!"

The king said to her, "Don't be afraid. What do you see?" The woman said, "I see a spirit coming up out of the ground."

"What does he look like?" he asked. "An old man wearing a robe is coming up," she said. Then Saul knew it was Samuel, and he bowed down and prostrated himself with his face to the ground.

Samuel said to Saul, "Why have you disturbed me by bringing me up?" "I am in great distress,"

Saul said. "The Philistines are fighting against me, and God has turned away from me. He no longer answers me, either by prophets or by dreams. So I have called on you to tell me what to do."

Samuel said, "Why do you consult me, now that the LORD has turned away from you and become your enemy?

The LORD has done what he predicted through me. The LORD has torn the kingdom out of your hands and given it to one of your neighbors—to David. Because you did not obey the LORD or carry out his fierce wrath against the Amalekites, the LORD has done this to you today. The LORD will hand over both Israel and you to the Philistines, and tomorrow you and your sons will be with me. The LORD will also hand over the army of Israel to the Philistines." **1 Samuel 28:8-19**

A program on the History Channel titled "In Search of —" on Tuesday August 29, 2000 did a segment on "Spirit Photography". While much of it proved to be a hoax, there were credible instances where careful scientific investigation could not disprove the validity of the photographic spirit image.

I've just made a case for the substantive nature of some hyperdimensional "spiritual beings". It speaks of Samuel in substantive terms. One might be curious as to what a photograph of Saul's encounter with Samuel, taken by a sophisticated state of the art camera, would show?

There's an inordinate interest by the general public in all things psychic. It's obvious that the motivation is the same that Eve experienced when Satan said, *"God doth know that in the day ye eat thereof, then your eyes shall be opened, and ye shall be as gods."* The universal desire to have God's power to perceive the supernatural for selfish reasons is still just as real today as it was in the Garden of Eden.

Ouija boards, tarot cards, palmistry, fortune telling and astrology have a sufficient element of validity about them to trap the unwary. They must be recognized as a tool of Satan to tempt the gullible into a trap of disobedience, and to do something God abhors. *"Anyone who does these things is detestable to the LORD."* **Deuteronomy 18:12**

The slippery slope:

There is legitimate research in parapsychology going on in universities around the world. Duke University, where I

went to school, was a pioneer in this field. The University of
California, Berkeley was the first accredited American university to give a Ph.D. in parapsychology. Stanford and
other major universities have conducted research projects on
telepathy, psychokinesis and clairvoyance (remote viewing).
Metaphysics is a two-edged sword, because to the carnal
world it validates the existence of supernatural reality. It
also lends credibility to genuine, spiritual Christian experience.

It furnishes tools for some frightening, sinful abuse. The
Russians have been experimenting with these capabilities in
an effort to exercise remote behavior control and the manipulation of individuals thousands of miles away.[1] In a book
by Ostrander and Schroeder, (Prentice Hall) entitled *Psychic
Discoveries Behind the Iron Curtain*, wild assertions are
made about accomplishments by the use of psychic powers.
My personal feeling is that most of these reports are wild ex-
aggerations. Nevertheless, it is troublesome to wonder how
much truth is buried in the fiction.

I'm sure most of my readers have had some sort of spontaneous psychic experience. This has been true in my life,
and so let me try to put these experiences into a reasonable
perspective. By doing so, we should be able to separate the
good and the indifferent from the bad.

One day, I was invited to give a talk at a Rotary Club
luncheon. The topic I chose for my talk was parapsychology.
Following the meeting a prominent business man came up to
me and said, "Dr. Nesbitt, could you take a few minutes to
listen to an experience I had awhile back?".

"Certainly," I answered.

"I've never told anyone about this before because I was
afraid they would either think I'm crazy, or made it up. A
little over a year ago, I awoke early one morning. It was too
early to get up, and as I lay there in bed I sort of dozed off.
In this light sleep I had a terrible nightmare. I saw my son
lying in the gutter unconscious with his bicycle crumpled
beside him.

---

[1] The Mind Race,Targ & Harary, Dust Cover

I awoke with my heart pounding. It was a little after seven. I got out of bed, dressed and ate a light breakfast. Before leaving for work, I checked my son's room to reassure myself that he was all right. He was still sound asleep and seemed to be fine.

At work I couldn't concentrate; the picture of my son lying unconscious in the gutter filled me with fear. A few minutes after nine a coworker stuck his head in the door and said, 'Jack you better come out here there's been an accident.' I ran to the front door of my office and looked out at the street. There was my son lying unconscious in the gutter with the front wheel of his bike crumpled just as in the dream. In fact, everything I saw was exactly as it was in the dream. The dream was a photographic image of what met my eyes when I looked out the door.

Because of my preoccupation with my dream I had left some important papers at home, and my son was bringing them to me. When he stopped in front of my office, a car hit him. Fortunately, he was not critically injured. He had a concussion and multiple scrapes and bruises. He was out of the hospital in a few days and he has been fine ever since."

Researchers have collected hundreds of anecdotal experiences like this one. This type of evidence is not scientifically acceptable to authenticate the validity of the phenomena of precognition and that is why so many universities have been doing research on the subject. Duke University did a convincing study that psi (psychic phenomena) exists, but they were unable to demonstrate a universal replication of their findings that satisfied the physical scientists. The nearest confirmation of psi (psychic abilities) that I know of is described in the Stanford Research Institute experiments with 'remote viewing'[2] In these experiments, one experimenter would travel to an unspecified location. The remote viewer would then draw a picture of what the experimenter was seeing. There was a high degree of correlation between the site location and the picture drawn by the remote viewer. The results were so im-

[2] The Mind Race, Targ and Harary

pressive the United States Army funded a research grant to see if this phenomenon would be useful in their intelligence operations. The research is described, in detail, in a book entitled, "*The Mind Race*", by Targ and Harary.

Every now and then para-psychological phenomena occur spontaneously without any obvious effort or meaning to the person involved. It's these kinds of events for which science would like to find an explanation. From a standpoint of hyper- dimensional theory the explanation of the event is readily understood. However, control over the event is not within the endowed power of the individual. Power to manipulate the events of time and space is only given by God, or by evil powers.

I've had several spiritual experiences that would be classified as parapsychological (I hope the semantic implication of this term does not give the wrong impression). These events are consistent with conservative theological teaching and practice. The following is an example of one of my experiences.

When I lived in Berkeley, CA, I had a friend named Lewis. He was about seven years older than I, but we had a lot of common interests, and we spent hours discussing theology, philosophy and science. He was an ordained minister, but he had not accepted a regular pastorate, so he had a lot of discretionary time. Our personal interaction ended when I left California to go to Duke University in North Carolina. Neither of us liked to write letters, and so except for the obligatory Christmas card we had no contact with one another. Three years went by, and for no obvious reason, I awoke one morning with troubling apprehension about Lewis. I sat down and wrote him a letter telling him of my concern and that I was praying for him.

An answer came back by return mail.

"Bill, its interesting you should write me at this time. I have been having trouble with my voice and the doctor told me a few days ago I may have to give up the ministry, because my voice may be permanently damaged."

Several more letters were exchanged between us and then one day a letter came containing the following information: "X-rays reveal my voice problem is due to a malignancy of my spine. I'm scheduled for surgery next week."

Several weeks later I got a letter saying Lewis had died.

God let me know of Lewis' need by laws He had instituted before the beginning of time; laws just as real and absolute as the laws of gravity. There is a place for hyperdimensional reality that both the scientist and the Christian are loath to acknowledge because it does not seem to conform to natural laws.

*Sci*entists are spending millions of dollars to build instruments to detect signs of intelligent life in the distant reaches of the universe. The sad part is that they are pointing their instruments in the wrong direction. All the reports of flying saucers indicate that (if such things exist) they appear suddenly and disappear suddenly. Neither radar nor other electronic devices can follow them when they disappear from view. The obvious conclusion is that if such objects exist they come through a time warp, or a wormhole, from another dimension, not from some distant galaxy.

In **Genesis** Chapter **6**, we read about the sons of God coming down to marry the daughters of men. This intermingling apparently resulted in an epidemic of sin so great that God sent the flood to wipe out all of humanity, except for Noah and his family. Since then the free mingling of "the sons of God," who I believe were children of Eve, born before she sinned, were no longer permitted by God to visit the earth, unless on specific assignment. However this does not mean these 'sons of God' disappeared. God quarantined the earth so the thing that happened before the flood wouldn't happen again.

I believe the Bible clearly teaches that extra-terrestrials both good and bad exist and that they have made visits to earth, both historically and in contemporary times. *"Do not forget to entertain strangers, for by so doing some people have entertained angels without knowing it." **Hebrews 13:2***

*" And Elisha prayed, "O LORD, open his eyes so he may see." Then the LORD opened the servant's eyes, and he looked and saw the hills full of horses and chariots of fire all around Elisha." **2 Kings 6:17***

Oh that we would have the faith and vision of Elisha. You may never see the invisible, but you will know it is there if you look up into the higher dimensions with the eyes of your spiritual body.

Chapter Eight
Believing The Impossible

The lights grew dim; the room became silent. On the platform, a man in his stocking feet, stood on a polished stainless steel drum. In his hands was an ordinary four-foot 2X4 with a narrow strip of metal foil running up one side. He carefully adjusted his position on the drum and held the 2x4 vertically over his head with both hands, fingers pointing upward. Then, in a tense voice, he said, 'READY"

Small streaks of lightning flowed from his fingertips as thousands of volts of static electricity flowed over his body and ran up the strips of metal foil on the piece of wood. Suddenly, the wood burst into flame, and the man shouted, 'OFF' The man was Irwin Moon, director of the Moody Bible Institute of Science.

He was giving a demonstration at the 1939 San Francisco World Fair. Thousands of people flocked to his presentations and saw there were natural laws of God that could accomplish things they thought were impossible.

The message from the demonstration was a powerful one. The physical demonstration showed that a human body can transmit the tremendous electrical power needed to set a wooden 2x4 on fire. But this is nothing compared to what Jesus did. From his hands, nailed to a wooden cross, flowed infinite spiritual power from the living God, setting the world on fire. A person willing to prepare himself to use the awesome power of God can also set his own world on fire, but to do this there is a condition to be met before God will permit a person to be a conduit for such spiritual energy. There can be no unforgiven sin in that person's life.

I was a personal friend of Irwin Moon, and he told me of an instance when he was not as prepared for this demonstration as he should have been. One of the absolute safety requirements is to be sure you have no metal on your body or in your clothing. He always removed his watch, wedding ring, coins etc. prior to mounting the stainless steel drum, but one night he overlooked his car keys. When he said READY, the car keys became white hot, burned a hole in his pocket and dropped to the floor. He swears he yelled OFF before the word READY was out of his mouth.

Sin, like the keys in Irwin Moon's pocket, is incompatible in one's life if he wants to transmit the awesome spiritual power of God.

Almost everyday scientists are doing things that were previously thought to be impossible. Because we are prone to sin God has put a limit on the amount of His power available to us. Scientists have conceded that there are some things that are theoretically possible, but that the power to accomplish them is probably beyond our capability. For instance, the ability to physically explore higher dimensions is thought to involve amounts of energy that are beyond our ability to produce. But just because we can't visualize something doesn't mean it doesn't exist; nor does it mean God doesn't do things we can't verify visually, or scientifically. *"With God all things are possible."* **Matthew 19:26** An essential part of our Christian faith is to recognize God's power is not limited, and He is capable of managing any, and every problem we can possibly have. Furthermore, He will entrust us with much of that power as our faith dictates and we are prepared to receive.

"Jesus looked at them and said, "With man this is impossible, but not with God; all things are possible with God." **Mark 10:27**

"Jesus replied, "I tell you the truth, if you have faith and do not doubt, not only can you do what was done to the fig tree, but also you can say to this mountain, 'Go, throw yourself into the sea,' and it will be done. If you believe, you will receive whatever you ask for in prayer."' **Matthew 21:21**

"He replied, "Because you have so little faith. I tell you the truth, if you have faith as small as a mustard seed, you can

say to this mountain, 'Move from here to there' and it will move. Nothing will be impossible for you." **Matthew 17:20**

These statements have been interpreted as symbolic, and so they are for the most part, but from a standpoint of hyperdimensional theory they can be taken literally. For instance, Mona Loa, on the big island of Hawaii is over ten thousand feet high. God, by reversing the passage of time for that particular object, can make it disappear instantly into the ocean. Since God is not a prisoner of time, as we are, He can accomplish this with ease without breaking any natural laws, except the one He invoked on mankind as a punishment for sin. (The passage of time) As described in our story of Timescape Explorer, God sees the time-space plane from a hyperdimensional point of view. Mono Loa rose out of the ocean as a result of volcanic eruption, and in the "NOW" of the past that event is still occurring. God can, by reversing our time perception, cause the mountain to disappear beneath the waves just by running the time tape backwards. You can do things like this on your video player; God who is the creator of 'time' can do it in actuality.

We must always keep in mind our faith is to accomplish God's will, not ours. Faith will not work for our own gratification. We can count on God's promises because —*"God did this so that, by two unchangeable things in which it is impossible for God to lie, we who have fled to take hold of the hope offered to us may be greatly encouraged."* **Hebrews 6:18**   But remember, — *"without faith it is impossible to please God, because anyone who comes to him must believe that he exists and that he rewards those who earnestly seek him."* **Hebrews 11:6**

As Christians we need to understand what is possible and what isn't. Much of what we view as impossible is due to ignorance or lack of faith. Hopefully understanding hyperdimensional theory will reduce our ignorance and increase our faith.

Over the years, many of the things science has said were impossible have either become theoretically possible or have actually been physically demonstrated. Higher dimensions have passed from the limbo of speculation to the realm of serious scientific investigation. The irony is that scientists think they have discovered something new, and fail to realize God created it the way they found it, before the world began.

As scientists make these amazing discoveries, paradoxically, they confirm the concepts set forth in the Bible thousands of years ago. The theories of hyperdimensions provide a logical explanation for many events in the Bible that are difficult to understand. A recent discovery expanding our understanding of the Bible is reported in the journal *Nature*.

For generations, physicists believed nothing could go faster than the speed of light moving through a vacuum - a speed of 186,000 miles per second, but in an experiment in Princeton, N.J., physicists sent a pulse of laser light through a chamber of cesium vapor at 310 times the speed of light. The unbelievable thing about this experiment is that the pulse of laser light traveled so fast it exited the chamber before it had finished entering it. The explanation proposed by the investigators is that the leading edge of the laser beam has all the information needed to produce the pulse on the other side of the chamber, so the entire pulse does not need to reach the chamber for it to exit the other side. Dr. Wang, one of the researchers said, that this is only possible because light has no mass; this could not be done with physical objects.

Dr. Raymond Chiao, a physicist at the University of California, Berkeley, who was not involved in the experiment, said this is a breakthrough because people thought such a thing was impossible. This experiment tests Einstein's limits of relativity developed nearly a century ago.

I would like to propose a theory I've developed about time and the speed of light, based purely on logic. As far as I know, there is no credible scientific support to confirm my assumptions, so you must judge whether my unproved theory is logical. Previous assertions of mine, concerning the application of scientific theories to the Bible, have been based on creditable theoretical evidence proposed by recognized scientists. References are cited for those assumptions.

I've already proposed a theory of creation different from traditional concepts; now I'm going to propose another idea I've never heard expressed before, and how these ideas have helped me understand some mysterious events in the Bible.

With this disclaimer, I would like to propose that time has a determinable theoretical linear speed across the time-space plane, similar to light. This assumption is partially based on a statement made by Fred Wolf, a Ph.D. in Theoretical Physics. He asks, "How fast do we go through time?" His answer is, "at the speed of light." I believe time proceeds at a speed a little faster than the speed of light; perhaps at 200,000 linear time-space miles per second.

The basis for this assumption is as follows: A linear time line runs from past to future. Intersecting this time-space line and at right angles to it is another line we call the present, or "NOW" (In our previous discussion, the linear time-space line, from past to future, is referred to as the fourth dimension and the intersecting line is referred to as the fifth dimension.)

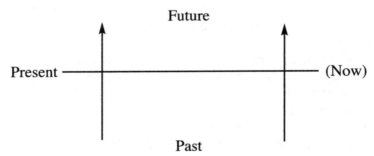

Figure Nine

The horizontal line represents the "NOW" of our sensory perception. It progresses from past to future at a constant speed that we measure in seconds, minutes, hours, etc., but it also has a linear speed through time-space that exceeds the speed of light. A pulse of light leaving its source in the present has to travel laterally in time-space to reach its target. If the wave/photon is slower than the forward speed of time it won't reach its target until a sufficient length of time has passed.

In quantum physics, a subatomic particle can be manipulated so it will appear to an observer at two separate physical locations in space at the same time. The only logical explanation to explain this phenomenon is for the particle to travel laterally in time-space at the linear speed of time. By doing so it maintains a constant identity in the present and it can be seen simultaneously at more than one point anywhere along the lateral time-space line of the present.

The next step is to see if a pulse of energy can be forced to exceed the speed of time, and if so what would happen? The laser-cesium gas chamber experiment answered that question for me. In this experiment, the speed of the laser pulse was measured at 310 times the speed of light. By exceeding the speed of time it was able to leave the chamber while still in the process of entering it. The significant part of this is that the pulse of light has entered the forbidden area of the past; that Einstein and other classical physicists have said was impossible, although admitting that the past still must physically exist.

Dr. Lijun Wang, a researcher with the private NEC Institute, said, 'This effect can not be used to send information back in time.' This statement indicates the thought had crossed his mind that the laser beam had broken the time barrier and entered 'time past'.

However, logic tells us if the speed of time is slower than the speed of the laser pulse, and if the laser pulse started at zero and was moving laterally at 310 x 180,000 miles per second, toward a target that was moving forward at 200,000 (+) or (-) miles per second, it would reach the target before the target area reached a visual position on the lateral time-space line we call the present. Therefore, it would be able to enter the target, pass through it, and be seen in the present leaving the chamber before it was seen entering the chamber.

Theologically, this is important because it demonstrates there are times when God uses the hyperdimensional past as a resource to solve our problem with guilt. The way God forgives our sin is by entering the past and actually wiping out our sins as if they had never been committed. *"I have swept away your offenses like a cloud, your sins like the morning mist."* **Isaiah 44:22**

It's interesting that many scientists have no trouble believing in obscure and complicated theories, and yet fail to recognize the obvious indications that the universe is designed, created and operated by a being of incomprehensible wisdom, unimaginable power, and unfathomable love for that which He has created. Some scientists criticize the Christian for believing in God and intelligent design. They think what the Christian believes is impossible, and yet they believe a much more impossible scenario; namely that the highly complex universe, and life on earth happened by chance and random undirected development.

From the standpoint of pure logic, the intelligent design scenario is more consistent with the observable evidence. As a matter of fact, the new concepts of time and space cast further doubt on Darwinian evolution. The illusion of time and motion is created by our perception being limited to the immediate time-space landscape over which we're passing.

If we live in a static universe, then evolution is impossible; evolution can't occur if there is no motion. The "long bodies" of all created life are already present in the past, present and future, to the end of time.

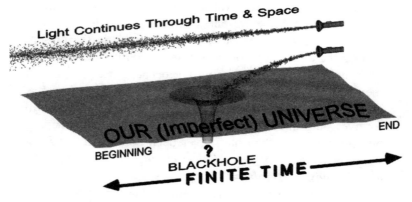

Figure Ten

Normally a beam of light continues in a straight line through time and space, but light, like time is affected by gravity. Gravity will bend both time and light. When a beam of light approaches a black hole the pull of gravity becomes so strong that the beam of light ceases to trave in a parallel path across the time-space plane and is pulled vertically across the event horizon of the black hole and both time and the light cease to exist Eternity without the passage of time occurs at the center of a black hole.

Scientists have discovered that there are numerous places in our universe where "time" has stopped and eternity without time is a reality (see Fig. 10). This is similar to the state of time-lessness we will experience in the heareafter. The timelessness is the same, but the physical environment will be vastly different.

Chapter Nine
True Lies

It happened in the Garden of Eden one bright sunny day, and I picture the scenario something like this:

"Hi Eve, How are things going?"

"Just fine; I'm so happy, things couldn't be better."

"There're some beautiful trees around here, does God let you eat the fruit from them?"

"Oh yes, we can eat as much as we want from any of the trees except that one over there in the middle of the garden."

"Why is that?"

"Because, He said if we eat that fruit, or even touch it, we'll die."

" *Now the serpent was more crafty than any of the wild animals the LORD God had made. He said to the woman, "Did God really say, 'You must not eat from any tree in the garden'?"* **Genesis 3:1**

The serpent burst out laughing, "You don't believe that do you? You will not surely die. (A half-truth.) What he didn't add was "right away."

In other words, what the serpent was saying was that there was no poison in the fruit; it didn't contain arsenic, or some other lethal toxic substance that would kill them. Which was true. With insidious cleverness he had told a true lie. What he accomplished by this dialog was more than just getting Eve to disobey God; he set the clock running that would determine a time of death from then on for every human. Before that day there was no passing of time, only the glorious state of living in an eternal "NOW."

God knows if you eat the fruit from that tree your eyes will be opened and you will know good and evil just like He does." (A truthful part of the true lie.)

"*When the woman saw that the fruit of the tree was good for food and pleasing to the eye, and also desirable for*

gaining wisdom, she took some and ate it. She also gave some to her husband, who was with her, and he ate it."
Genesis 3:6

If we understand the psycho dynamics of Eve's temptation we should be able to deal more intelligently with the temptations in our daily life. The Bible defined the elements of the personality thousands of years before Freud was born. But Freud has given us a much more detailed analysis of the reasons Eve acted as she did, so let us look briefly at Eve's problem from a standpoint of Freudian psychiatry. Even though many of Freud's ideas have been abandoned, I believe his theory of the basic elements of the personality are still useful.

He proposed that the personality is divided into the id, ego, and superego. The id is concerned with satisfying unconscious biological drives such as hunger, sex, sleep, the avoidance of pain and other noxious stimuli. In this case, she saw the tree was good for food. Even though she was surrounded with many good things to eat, the id still desired to eat whatever appealed to that desire. In a moment, we will see why this is an important part of her failure to obey God.

The ego basically mediates between the consciousness of the individual and the reality of the world around him. The ego is primarily narcissistic, which means objects exist primarily for its satisfaction and pleasure, and it desires to incorporate that pleasure into one's self. Another important part of the ego is its feeling of omnipotence: being all powerful and all important. These aspects of the personality are easily recognized in a baby.

Again we see the psychodynamics of the situation working in Eve's mind. The fruit was pleasant to the eye, imposing a classical ego reason for yielding to the temptation. This is a significant motivational desire if the basic demands of the id have been met. But remember that Adam and Eve were in an environment of indescribable beauty. In addition, they had prestige and power beyond anything modern man can achieve. *"God blessed them and said to them, 'Be fruitful and increase in number; fill the earth and subdue it.*

Rule over the fish of the sea and the birds of the air and over every living creature that moves on the ground.'" **Genesis 1:28** Yet she wanted more.

Had the temptation stopped there she might have resisted it, and the history of the human race would be substantially different, but she still had to deal with the superego, the most powerful of the three parts of the personality.

The superego is composed of two parts. The first is the image of hated or feared objects and actions. This is a negative function and is represented by conscience. The second part of the superego is the 'ego ideal', represented by status seeking, and this is considered a positive function. It's the basis for ambition, personal recognition, social status, and self worth. The most powerful of the three temptations was the appeal to the ego-ideal side of her superego. This may have been the only part of the superego that existed, because it's unlikely that conscience had developed. There was no need for conscience until then because conscience deals with the consequences of selfishness, and failures to meet the expectations of others. Up until the fall, Adam and Eve were perfect; they had not yet yielded to temptation; therefore, they met the expectations of God with enthusiasm.

It's amazing that long before Freud the Bible recognized these traits of the human personality, and if we understand them the completeness of our salvation can be better understood. One can only conjecture what went through Eve's mind, but one might wonder whether the fact that she was created from man as a companion for him rather than being created first, or even at the same time, was a factor in wanting to improve her status, and this became the temptation she couldn't resist. Whatever the reason, the idea of achieving an attribute of God, achieving higher status, thus improving her self-worth, was an overwhelming desire of her superego.

So even though there was truth in the serpent's statement, the lie drove her into the fatal act of disobedience to God. We have lived with the consequence of that act of disobedience ever since. Everyday of our life we struggle with the temptations faced by Eve, and we have no better success in resisting them. Our id makes us eat more than we should, seek comfort when we should be working and at inappropriate times become involved in thoughts and acts of sex. We lust for beauty beyond our means. More important needs may be neglected for jewelry, clothes, cars and recreation to meet our ego's narcissistic desires. And our superego will sacrifice marriage, family, health and security for fame, prestige and feelings of self worth. Men will lie, steal and compromise their moral ideals to achieve their goals of status within their peer group. Sadly, when they achieve those goals they find they're not enough and they want more. The superego is the home of *pride*, and pride is an abomination to God.

"*To fear the LORD is to hate evil; I hate pride and arrogance, evil behavior and perverse speech.*" **Proverbs 8:13** "*When pride comes, then comes disgrace, but with humility comes wisdom.*" **Proverbs 11:2** "*Pride goes before destruction, a haughty spirit before a fall.*" **Proverbs 16:18** "*The pride of your heart has deceived you.*" **Obadiah 1:3** "*The LORD detests all the proud of heart. Be sure of this: They will not go unpunished.*" **Proverbs 16:5**

The lie is still being whispered in the ears of those who will listen. "The benefits are greater than the penalties. You're not really going to have to pay the price." When a lie was coupled with a truth, especially a lie that negates any bad consequences from believing something you want to believe, one is more inclined to accept the true part and ignore the lie. Frequently, we fail to realize what Eve did had to be undone by Jesus, the Son of God.

In order to appreciate the humanness of Jesus, and that He also had to deal with the identical temptations that caused Eve to fall, we should remember He had to experience the very same temptations Eve had, but magnified thousands of times.

In Matthew, the fourth chapter the first ten verses, we have an account of this ordeal. Jesus had the same elements to His personality that we have and the temptations He

suffered were just as real as those Eve or any of us have
suffered.

*"Then Jesus was led by the Spirit into the desert to be
tempted by the devil. After fasting forty days and forty
nights, he was hungry. The tempter came to him and said,
"If you are the Son of God, tell these stones to become
bread."* ***Matthew 4:1-10*** (The id temptation of Jesus was
just as real and much more powerful than the one Eve had to
face. Jesus had not eaten for forty days and was weak and
hungry from lack of food.)

*Jesus answered, "It is written: 'Man does not live on
bread alone, but on every word that comes from the mouth
of God.'"*

*Then the devil took him to the holy city and had him
stand on the highest point of the temple. "If you are the Son
of God," he said, "throw yourself down. For it is written:
"'He will command his angels concerning you, and they will
lift you up in their hands, so that you will not strike your
foot against a stone.'"*. (This was a classical ego temptation.
As mentioned above, a powerful drive of the ego is for omnipotence. What better way could Jesus prove His
omnipotence than by jumping off the temple and not be
harmed. If He could walk on the water without sinking He
had the power to do this.)

*Jesus answered him, "It is also written: 'Do not put the
Lord your God to the test.'"*

*Again, the devil took him to a very high mountain and
showed him all the kingdoms of the world and their
splendor. "All this I will give you," he said, "if you will bow
down and worship me."*

*Jesus said to him, "Away from me, Satan! For it is
written: 'Worship the Lord your God, and serve him only.'"*
Matthew 4:1-10 As with Eve, the temptation of the
superego was the crucial one. Here was an opportunity to
develop a world dynasty of unrivaled greatness without the
pain and suffering of the cross. Satan had the power to give
this to Him, and by yielding, a façade of success would be
established that would go down in history as a kingdom

greater than Solomon's: an unparalleled era of world peace and prosperity that would be unique. He would be a king on a magnificent throne with unlimited power, not a homeless itinerant teacher. But we would be lost in our sin, damned for eternity. There would be no second chance to redeem humanity from the clutches of the destroyer. The awesome power of the love of God gave Jesus the strength to say no to the same temptations to which Eve, in her weakness, had yielded.

God does not want us to suffer the consequences that come from yielding to temptation and so He broke the spell of Satan's power by sending His Son to prove temptations of the flesh and of the mind, could be conquered by simple faith and obedience to God. Sin entered into the world through a woman and was partaken of by man. God, in His infinite mercy and kindness, brought salvation into the world through a woman (man had nothing to do with it) and man again, because of the woman, is able to partake of the salvation that was provided. *"She will give birth to a son, and you are to give him the name Jesus, because he will save his people from their sins."* **Matthew 1:21**

Critics say if Jesus was divine He couldn't understand the temptations of man. If He were human, on the other hand, then He was nothing more than a good man, and His crucifixion was nothing more than a martyr's death. This kind of thinking shows a complete misunderstanding of the created capabilities of humankind.

Jesus was born as human as any other man. He had a spirit-soul at His birth as innocent as Adam and Eve's when they were created. But Jesus did not separate himself from God by disobedience, as Adam and Eve did. It's important to realize that Jesus had the same potential to sin as Adam and Eve. If He didn't, He wouldn't have been tempted. The one big difference is that Adam and Eve were in a perfect sinless environment when they were tempted, while Jesus was born into an environment steeped in sin.

Jesus, in spite of the human limitations he assumed, lived a perfect life and maintained an unbroken relationship with

God. By doing this He demonstrated the capabilities humans could have if they completely trusted God. The miracles He performed were done within the framework of our human capabilities. We have the capability of letting God work through us to accomplish things considered impossible to natural man. *"I tell you the truth, anyone who has faith in me will do what I have been doing. He will do even greater things than these, because I am going to the Father. And I will do whatever you ask in my name, so that the Son may bring glory to the Father. You may ask me for anything in my name, and I will do it."* **John 14:12-14**

✦   ✦   ✦   ✦   ✦

Some scientists are guilty of half-truth deceptions. They tell us about the wonders and the precision of the universe (a marvelous truth) and then try to tell us there was no divine intelligence behind it. They say a single cell is unbelievably complex, (true), but life started spontaneously from a primeval prebiotic soup; a theory that has recently been disproved, and that everything, including man, is a product of blind chance development directed toward the selection of the fittest, also a lie. They would like us to believe the lie along with the truth about the marvels of our universe.

Christians sometimes become confused by the proclamations of science and their apparent conflict with the Bible. The reason is that part of what the scientists are saying is true, but many times they are telling us half-truths and their conclusions are false. It's important to distinguish between the facts of science and the conclusions scientists draw from them. A number of conclusions can be derived from different interpretations of the same data, and scientists choose conclusions that more nearly conform to their belief systems. If they don't believe in God, they obviously do not consider divine factors in reaching those conclusions.

A good example of a scientific true lie is a scientific analysis of 'falling in love'. I can best explain this with a short allegory.

Bob and Jim had been pals since they could first walk. They played together, enjoyed the same games, toys, books and movies. They went to the same school, had the same friends and were inseparable. Both were extremely bright and both of them wanted to do scientific research.

In their last year of high school, something happened that was very disturbing to Jim. Bob was losing interest in doing things with him and he seemed to be in a sort of daze. It was a happy daze; in fact, Bob seemed to be floating on a rosy cloud. The only thing that could account for this change was a friendship Bob had developed with a beautiful, vivacious high school cheerleader.

Jim confided his concerns with his parents.

His father laughed and said, "Bob's perfectly normal; he's just fallen in love."

But Jim couldn't understand why this could make so much difference in his relationship with Bob, and being sure there must be a scientific reason for this change, he went to the university near his home and asked for an appointment with the head of the Department of Psychology. He was able to get an appointment with Dr. Brainwash, a friend of his father, who was a professor of neurophysiology.

Dr. Brainwash was a kindly old gentleman with many years of experience in the study of the brain and its functions He was an entrenched pragmatist when it came to the chemistry and function of the human brain.

In answer to Jim's questions, he explained in detail what was going on in Bob's head. He told him about the neuroanatomy, the biochemical reactions, the neurons, axons, the hillocks and the synapses. He described the chemical reactions mediating emotional response and even showed him P.E.T. Scans (Positive Emission Tomography) pictures of the activity of the brain.

Jim knew that everything Dr. Brainwash told him was true and concluded his friend Bob had a chemical imbalance in his brain, from which he hoped he would soon recover.

A few weeks later, Jim went to a church youth party and met Lisa. His talk with Dr. Brainwash evaporated like the fog of his breath on a cold mirror. Fireworks were set off in his brain. Rockets, roman candles and sparklers lighted a feeling of ecstasy that made him feel weak all over.

Now he understood Bob's behavior, not because of the scientific explanation of Dr. Brainwash, which was a gigantic true lie. Love was something much more important and real to him than scientific facts. He had the experience of falling in love and he knew exactly what had happened to Bob.

Being a Christian is like that. Psychologists, sociologists, theologians and philosophers can tell you true lies by reciting objective facts about Christianity, but all their combined knowledge fades into insignificance in the aura of the love of Jesus Christ, the fellowship of the Holy Spirit and the feeling of awesome ecstasy of being a child of God.

Unfortunately ministers and tele-evangelists are telling Christians all over the world one of the cruelest of true lies. The subtle and convincing power of this true lie is that it is based on a partial understanding of an important body of scripture. The truth in the lie is based on *2 Corinthians 9:6* *"Whosoever sows sparingly will reap sparingly and whosoever sows generously will reap generously."*

Using this verse ministers of the Gospel perpetrate one of the most heinous lies ever uttered. They persuade people that if they give a little money they will get a lot of money in return by some divine act. They recount stories of listeners who gave fifty dollars in their poverty and received a thousand dollars in the mail the next day. People in dire financial situations are urged to scrape together what little they have and give it to a particular ministry with the assurance that God has said they will be rewarded with a hundred, or a thousand times the amount they have given.

If one looks analytically at this, those who interpret the scriptures to support their promises of great returns from the gift are perpetuating the identical temptation Satan used on Eve. Eve was tempted to be more like God for selfish reasons and not to be more God-like. What these ministers are really doing is encouraging people to play a heavenly slot machine. Put in enough money and you will hit the jackpot.

This is nothing more than pandering to a person's selfish nature. While it may not be true in all cases, in many situations the reason for giving is either consciously, or subconsciously a selfish act done for personal reward and not primarily for the benefit of the recipient of the gift.

Mark paints a good picture of this. *"As he taught,* Jesus said, *"Watch out for the teachers of the law. They like to walk around in flowing robes and be greeted in the market-places, and have the most important seats in the synagogues and the places of honor at banquets. They devour widows' houses and for a show make lengthy prayers. Such men will be punished most severely."* **Mark 12:38-40**

Some of the prominent tele-evangelists encourage people of limited means to give beyond a prudent level with the promise of selfish rewards. This is the very sin that Jesus is preaching against. The result is that the seed the giver thinks he is planting in fertile soil is falling on hard rocky ground and is being devoured by the vultures. Vultures in tailored suits, chauffeured limousines and Lear Jets. The economic, social, emotional and spiritual wreckage left behind them is horrifying.

Now let's look at the true meaning of sacrificial giving. It's one of the most rewarding acts carried out by the Christian when done in a Biblical way.

"Out of the most severe trial, their overflowing joy and their extreme poverty welled up in rich generosity. For I testify that they gave as much as they were able, and even beyond their ability. Entirely on their own, they urgently pleaded with us for the privilege of sharing in this service to the saints." **2 Corinthians 8:2** These people were not giving because they expected a great monetary reward; they were giving because they saw a need and as Christians felt obligated to do something about it. The thought of getting a lot more than they gave never entered their minds.

"Each man should give what he has decided in his heart to give, not reluctantly or under compulsion, for God loves a

cheerful giver. And God is able to make all grace abound to you, so that in all things at all times, having all that you need, you will abound in every good work. As it is written: "He has scattered abroad his gifts to the poor; his righteousness endures forever."

Now he who supplies seed to the sower and bread for food will also supply and increase your store of seed and will enlarge the harvest of your righteousness. You will be made rich in every way so that you can be generous on every occasion, and through us your generosity will result in thanksgiving to God.

This service that you perform is not only supplying the needs of God's people but is also overflowing in many expressions of thanks to God. Because of the service by which you have proved yourselves, men will praise God for the obedience that accompanies your confession of the gospel of Christ, and for your generosity in sharing with them and with everyone else." ***2 Corinthians 9:7-13***

"Give, and it will be given to you. A good measure, pressed down, shaken together and running over, will be poured into your lap. For with the measure you use, it will be measured to you." ***Luke 6:38*** The reward may not be in like kind and it only comes when done in the spirit God intended one to have. If the motive is selfish the reward is canceled.

"For if the willingness is there, the gift is acceptable according to what one has, not according to what he does not have. Our desire is not that others might be relieved while you are hard pressed, but that there might be equality. At the present time, your plenty will supply what they need, so that in turn their plenty will supply what you need. Then there will be equality, as it is written: "He who gathered much did not have too much, and he who gathered little did not have too little." ***2 Corinthians 8:12-15***

"And God is able to make all grace abound to you, so that in all things at all times, having all that you need, you will abound in every good work. As it is written: "He has scattered abroad his gifts to the poor; his righteousness endures forever." ***2 Corinthians 9:8-9***

*"Honor the LORD with your wealth, with the first fruits of all your crops; then your barns will be filled to overflowing, and your vats will brim over with new wine." **Proverbs 3:9–10***

It's my contention that God wants us to give out of love from the heart, not out of a desire to solve a financial problem of our own. If we are good stewards of what God has given us, He will supply our needs. It may not be with money, it may not even be with material blessings, but if the gift is given unselfishly the reward is absolutely certain.

I've been a Christian all my life. I know the Bible quite well, yet I've been guilty of the same foolish mistakes I'm accusing others of making. I remember embarking on several entrepreneurial adventures. In my stupidity, I told God if he would give me success in my endeavor I would give Him half of all my profits. The projects were miserable failures. As I look back on those misadventures, it reminds me of a child saying to his multimillionaire father, "Dad, if you give me twenty dollars, I'll give you back ten dollars."

An illustration of this principle is the observation made of the poor widow.

"Jesus sat down opposite the place where the offerings were put and watched the crowd putting their money into the temple treasury. Many rich people threw in large amounts. But a poor widow came and put in two very small copper coins, worth only a fraction of a penny.

Calling his disciples to him, Jesus said, 'I tell you the truth, this poor widow has put more into the treasury than all the others. They all gave out of their wealth; but she, out of her poverty, put in everything—all she had to live on.'"
Mark 12:41-44

The Bible says nothing about this poor woman receiving massive wealth for her sacrificial giving, but little did she know that in her abject poverty she would be teaching billions of people throughout the ages the secret of obtaining an unfathomable reward for her love and generosity toward God.

"And if you lend to those from whom you expect re-payment, what credit is that to you? Even 'sinners' lend to 'sinners,' expecting to be repaid in full. But love your

enemies, do good to them, and lend to them without ex-
pecting to get anything back. Then your reward will be
great, and you will be sons of the Most High, because he is
*kind to the ungrateful and wicked." **Luke 6:34-35***

I'm afraid many people consider their gift a loan to God
and expect exorbitant interest. From personal experience,
learned after years of ignorance, the joy of giving and the
rewards received from being a faithful steward far surpass
any monetary gain.

Chapter Ten
Understanding The Inconceivable

It is reported that Albert Einstein said, "Pure thought can grasp reality." Many of the theories of theoretical physics are based on mathematics, logic and pure thought. Hyperdimensional theory can't be proved, yet logic and abstract thinking have given credibility to the concept and it has been useful in understanding the invisible things in nature, such as time, dark matter, quarks and neutrinos. Scientists should have no objection to the Christian's using mathematics, pure thought and logic to support his or her belief in the Bible, even if these beliefs can't be scientifically proved.

The limitations of our five senses make it difficult for us to understand spiritual truths. However, by using information and techniques from theoretical physics, we can see a little more clearly what those truths might be.

A classic example of scientists asking us to understand the inconceivable is their proposal of the eleven dimensional "String Theory". Since it's not testable, it's not a real theory, but basically it states the universe was originally a eleven dimensional structure and at 0.000,000,000,000,000,000, 000,000,000,000,000,000,000,000,1 seconds after the big bang, the fabric of the universe ripped, and seven of the eleven dimensions rolled up into a ball too small to see, leaving the visible four dimensional universe that we can perceive.

By using the string theory, scientists can explain much they couldn't explain before. Utilizing the same kind of argument, we can explain much in the Bible that was not explainable before, by using some theories of theoretical physics.

+   +   +   +   +

Perhaps the most difficult dogma of the Christian Faith to understand is the concept of the Trinity. Most of the analogies that have been used to understand the Trinitarian God don't fit. "Water, steam and ice being one substance in three different forms" doesn't work, because the figures of the Godhead are not interchangeable, as are water, steam and ice. Another analogy, although close, is "Spirit, mind and body," but this doesn't work either, because the scriptures assigns specific attributes to each member of the Trinity that are not consistent with the interdependency of spirit, mind and body.

The analogy I like best is that of an electric light system. The three independent parts (the generator, the electricity, and the light) are identifiable as separate entities, but function together as a harmonious system. God the Father is the generator, and the source of the power. Jesus says he receives the power [of *the Holy Spirit*] from the Father.

*"And Jesus came and spake unto them, saying, All **power** is given unto me in heavenand in earth."* **Matthew 28:18** The Holy Spirit is the power [energy], *"Through mighty signs and wonders, by **the power of the Spirit of God**."* **Romans 15:19** *"He [John] was not that Light, but was sent to bear witness of that Light.[Jesus the Son]."* **John 8:12** *"When Jesus spoke again to the people,* he said, *"I am the **light** of the world."* **John 8:12** The power and the light are separate, identifiable entities, but neither one can exist without the generator.

Analogies are not perfect, so is there a better way to understand the Trinity, in a logical, scientific way? I think there is, and I believe hyperdimensional physics provides an answer consistent with the Scriptures.

In Chapter Two we discussed the fourth dimension, and the long body concept. With this theory, we see all humanity is physically connected. My three children are still physically connected to my wife and me through fertilized ova. There is no break in the linear fourth dimensional continuity of substance linking our bodies with the bodies of our children. Our children are not only linked to us physically, they are exclusive, genetic expressions of the characteristics they inherited from us. In **Genesis 2:24** it says, *"For this*

*reason a man will leave his father and mother and be united
to his wife, and they will become one flesh."*

The body of a child is a fulfillment of this statement. The
flesh of the mother and that of the father have become one
in the body of the child, and through the child they [father
and mother] have become one substance.

*"I am the true vine, and my Father is the gardener. He
cuts off every branch in me that bears no fruit, while every
branch that does bear fruit he prunes so that it will be even
more fruitful. You are already clean because of the word I
have spoken to you. Remain in me, and I will remain in you.
No branch can bear fruit by itself; it must remain in the
vine. Neither can you bear fruit unless you remain in me. I
am the vine; you are the branches. If a man remains in me
and I in him, he will bear much fruit; apart from me you can
do nothing. If anyone does not remain in me, he is like a
branch that is thrown away and withers; such branches are
picked up, thrown into the fire and burned."* **John 15:1-6**

This is more than an analogy. The human race is a vine-
like structure, going all the way back to Adam and Eve.
From a hyperdimensional standpoint, there is no break in the
continuity of the physical genetic structure that exists
between Adam and Eve and you. The references Jesus
makes to pruning and grafting are acts God is literally
carrying out on the genealogic tree of the human race.

Jesus is depicted as the trunk of the vine, going back to
Abraham, as a single physical fourth dimensional structure
that plays a very important part in God's plan. Throughout
the ages, the Hebrew race has maintained a certain degree of
integrity and identity in spite of persecution and worldwide
dissemination.

So how does the above discussion apply to the concept of
a Trinitarian monotheistic God?

When God created man, He created him from the dust of
the ground. *"The LORD God formed the man from the dust
of the ground and breathed into his nostrils the breath of
life, and the man became a living being."* **Genesis 2:7**

And mankind will return to the substance from which he was created. *"By the sweat of your brow you will eat your food until you return to the ground, since from it you were taken; for dust you are and to dust you will return."* **Genesis 3:19**

Even though individuals of the human race are all one substance, each person has a unique cognitive identity. Applying this same logic to God, we discern that Father, Son and Holy Spirit are of one substance, but each person of the Trinity has a unique cognitive identity not shared with the other members. This is clearly evidenced by statements of Jesus,

"No one knows about that day or hour, not even the angels in heaven, nor the Son, but only the Father." **Mark 13:3** *"Going a little farther, he fell with his face to the ground and prayed, 'My Father, if it is possible, may this cup be taken from me. Yet not as I will, but as you will.'"* **Matthew 26:39** *"About the ninth hour Jesus cried out in a loud voice, 'Eloi, Eloi, lama sabachthani?'—which means, 'My God, my God, why have you forsaken me?'"* **Matthew 27:46**

These verses, and many others, are clear evidence of a separate cognitive identity between God, the Father and God, the Son. The following verses indicate the Holy Spirit also has an independent cognitive identity.

"Jesus said, 'But when he, the Spirit of truth, comes, he will guide you into all truth. He will not speak on his own; he will speak only what he hears, and he will tell you what is yet to come.'" **John 16:13-14**

Our language does not contain an adequate vocabulary to describe the attributes of our Trinitarian God. However, using words with which I'm familiar, the closest I can come is to say the Trinity has unique substance different from humans in the context of the following definition: "something that has independent existence and (*acts or*) is acted upon by (*or resulting in*) causes (Philos)" [italics mine]."

The early church fathers identified the Trinity as the Logos (Word). *"In the beginning was the Word, and the Word was with God, and the Word was God. He was with God in the beginning Through him all things were made; without him nothing was made that has been made. In him was life, and that life was the light of men."* **John 1:1-4**

Using this definition, I maintain the Trinity is of one unique substance, limited solely to the Godhead, expresses itself in, and through, three separate, but complementary cognitive identities. The completely harmonious cognitive expressions of the three persons of the Trinity result in a single uniform identity.

"I and my Father are one." **John 10:30** *"Well said, teacher,"* the man replied. *"You are right in saying that God is one and there is no other but him."* **Mark 12:32** *"Yet for us there is but one God, the Father, from whom all things came and for whom we live; and there is but one Lord, Jesus Christ, through whom all things came and through whom we live."* **1 Corinthians 8:6** *"God is spirit, and his worshipers must worship in spirit and in truth."* **John 4:24** *"On that day you will realize that I am in my Father, and you are in me, and I am in you."* **John 14:20**

The unity (and singleness) of our one Trinitarian God is in divine substance, not in cognitive expression. There is nothing else in, or outside of creation, that partakes of that divine substance. *"Hear, O Israel: The LORD our God, the LORD is one."* **Deuteronomy 6:4**

While all of humanity is of a single substance (dust) and is physically joined together, the Trinitarian Godhead is joined together as a single unique divine substance different from that of humanity.

Hopefully, the concept of the unity of different parts, through the continuity of higher dimensional connections, will help you understand how the three persons of the Trinity can be one.

But there is something more to this doctrine that is totally incomprehensible. It's a truth beyond the capability of the human mind to understand. God, unique in identity, so loved the world that He gave His only son, part of His own divine substance, to be joined in physical union with the dust of humanity. *"The Word became flesh and made his dwelling among us. We have seen his glory, the glory of the One and Only, who came from the Father, full of grace and truth."* **John 1:14**

He did not limit His union to the best of humanity. It was not limited to kings or presidents, or to Nobel or Pulitzer Prize winners, or to Rhodes Scholars, or Ph.Ds, but He offered this union to anyone of the human race willing to recognize their deplorable sinful state and accept His unmerited gift of redemption. Drunkards, prostitutes, thieves, and beggars were offered the gift of eternal life on the same basis as anyone else.

How could this happen? Jesus, the creator of the universe, maker of heaven and earth, willingly permitted himself to be shackled in a body of sinful flesh, submitted himself to the mockery and abuse by those He had formed from dust and then willingly died a horrible death, on a cross, for the sins of reprobate humanity. Can you imagine how He must have felt as He looked at the world, the vast expanse of the sky with the billions of stars He had created and cast into the unfathomable reaches of space. Why did He do it?

I would like to paint a fantasy picture of what I perceive might have happened.

✦   ✦   ✦   ✦   ✦

Within the perimeter of x-dimensional time-space an interesting conversation was in progress.

"Father, I would like to create a place of exceptional grandeur; a fabric of dark blue, studded with great balls of light, hung in the vast emptiness of elementary time-space. In that fabric I want to place a small sphere; a place of beauty and intricate design, with forested hills and verdant valleys, broad rivers and deep oceans. On this sphere, will be living creatures great and small and we will call the little sphere earth; will you help me?

"That's an interesting project Son, We'll do it together."

"Now the earth was formless and empty, darkness was over the surface of the deep, and the Spirit of God was hovering over the waters." **Genesis 1:2**   *"And God said, 'Let the water teem with living creatures, and let birds fly above the earth across the expanse of the sky. God created the great creatures of the sea and every living and moving thing with which the water teems, according to their kinds, and every winged bird according to its kind.' And God saw that it was good. And God said, 'Let the earth bring forth grass, the herb yielding seed, and the fruit tree yielding fruit after his kind, whose seed is in itself, upon the earth:' and it was so.*

"God made the wild animals according to their kinds, the livestock according to their kinds, and all the creatures that move along the ground according to their kinds. And God saw that it was good." **Genesis 1: 22-25**

God's son looked at the vast universe, and the little sphere they named Earth, and He said to his Father; "It's beautiful, more beautiful than I imagined it would be, but something more needs to be added."

"And what would that be?" His Father asked.

His son answered, "Father, I love you beyond my ability to express it, and your love for me is beyond comprehension. It's so fantastic I would like to expand it to include others with the capability to experience and return our love. It would not only expand our joy, but our love could be reciprocal, and the pleasure of sharing it would be multiplied many times over."

There was a pause, and a fleeting troubled look crossed His Father's face.

"You're right, but for this to occur, in the way you envision it, will cause you much pain. You're not familiar with pain, but if you're willing to endure the suffering such a project entails, the rewards will be beyond your greatest expectations."

"Why does there have to be suffering, Father? Can't we just create creatures that will love us the way we want them to."

"Yes, Son, We could, but that wouldn't accomplish what you desire. You don't want automatons that automatically love us because they're programmed to do so. Love, to be meaningful, must be voluntary, and in order to be voluntary the beings we create must have free will.

Our kingdom is built on immutable laws. Free will introduces the opportunity to break those laws, and that leads to pain and suffering. It's not our desire for anyone to suffer pain, but the integrity of our realm is dependent on strict conformity to its laws. The pain and suffering is not the consequence of a political decision, it's the result of trying to escape from the precision of the structure within which We exist. We saw the consequence of such disobedience when Satan and the rebellious angels tried to escape from the restraints of our government."

"And if We undertake the project as you envision it, what will be the rewards?"

"My Son, You want to love and be loved in the realms of ethereal ecstasy. The price is high, but there is nothing in heaven or on earth equal to that experience. Furthermore, those whom you choose will share in the indescribable experience. Are You sure you want to do it?"

" Father, it's my destiny, I must do it."

" *Then God said, 'Let us make man in our image, in our likeness.'*" **Genesis 1:26**

And so God created humans and He structured their personalities so they could experience the maximum pleasure possible from living.

"*The LORD God took the man and put him in the Garden of Eden to work it and take care of it.*" *And the LORD God commanded the man, "You are free to eat from any tree in the garden; but you must not eat from the tree of the knowledge of good and evil, for when you eat of it you will surely die.*" **Genesis 2:15-17**

But they disobeyed God and the terrible story of the battle with sin began. Because of fear they no longer relied on the love and protection of God, but sought refuge in selfish defensiveness. This isolation from God and self-protectiveness became a way of life for their children and their children' children.

"Father, what must I do now? This is a terrible tragedy."

First, we must prove to them they are incapable of restoring their lives to the perfection they have lost. Initially, we will let them see their conscience is not a reliable guide to restoring personal integrity. Then, we will give them a code of law by which to judge their behavior. They will soon see they can't live up to objective standards necessary for a safe and happy existence. Finally, they will realize their only hope is to turn to us for help. By recognizing their deplorable state and their inability to help themselves, some will confess their sins and pray to us for mercy and a restoration of fellowship. But they must understand the cost of such salvation, and when they do, it will be the seed of love that will grow into the thing you desire.

"Son, now it's time to demonstrate to our creation the true meaning of love. As you look at the genetic tree of civilization spreading out over the time-space plane, you will see some humans have the capability of responding to our love for them; others, by an act of their own free will, will, refuse. That's the peril of free will. You must choose those who will complete the plan we have set out to accomplish. *"For those God foreknew he also predestined to be conformed to the likeness of his Son, that he might be the firstborn among many brothers."* **Romans 8:29**

It's time for you to rescue those who are yours. Carefully select the ones you choose. You will be physically joining humanity with deity for now and all eternity. I have prepared a body for you to use to accomplish your task. *"Sacrifice and offering you did not desire, but a body you prepared for me."* **Hebrews 10:5** The Holy Spirit has prepared a beautiful virgin to incorporate your deity into humanity. She will be your mother. Her name is Mary. Your period of suffering is about to begin. You will be *"despised and rejected by men, a man of sorrows, and familiar with suffering."* **Isaiah 53:3** Through this experience you will learn that the ultimate understanding of Love is the price you are willing to pay to achieve it. And those who accept your salvation, from their deplorable state, will be born all over again and experience a love for You that is unfathomable.

And so, *" For what the law was powerless to do in that it was weakened by the sinful nature, God did by sending his own Son in the likeness of sinful man to be a sin offering. And so he condemned sin in sinful man."* **Romans 8:3** *"He was in the world, and though the world was made through him, the world did no recognize him. He came to that which was his own, but his own did not receive him. Yet to all who received him, to those who believed in his name, he gave the right to become children of God—children born not of natural descent, nor of human decision or a husband's will, but born of God. The Word became flesh and made his dwelling among us. We have seen his glory, the glory of the One and Only, who came from the Father, full of grace and truth."* **John 1:10-14**

How much does God love us?

" This is love: not that we loved God, but that he loved us and sent his Son as an atoning sacrifice for our sins." **John 4:10** *"For God so loved the world that he gave his one and only Son, that whoever believes in him shall not perish but have eternal life. For God did not send his Son into the world to condemn the world, but to save the world through him."* **John 3: 16-17**

The Son of God, creator of the universe, perfect in nature, perfect in wisdom, perfect in love, stooped to rescue filthy humanity, wash them clean with His very blood, clothe them in the garments of salvation, wrap them in the robe of His righteousness and present them to His Father as His betrothed bride.

The cost: rejection by many of those He came to save; mocked, scourged, humiliated, and forsaken by His friends, He went to an agonizing death. But the inconceivable part of His suffering was the relinquishing of the support of His

Father. *"About the ninth hour Jesus cried out in a loud voice, 'Eloi, Eloi, lama sabachthani?'—which means, 'My God, my God, why have you forsaken me?'"* **Matthew 27:46**

Jesus Christ paid the ultimate price to demonstrate His love for us. He gave up everything to demonstrate that His Love was of infinite magnitude. *"Greater love has no one than this, that he lay down his life for his friends."* **John 15:13**

It's our privilege to give up everything for Him and our reward is to experience the passion of His incomprehensible love for all eternity.

Chapter Eleven
Miracles Not Magic

I've seen death many times. I've struggled to start a heart that's stopped in sudden cardiac arrest. I've watched the line on the cardiac monitor go from normal sinus rhythm to ventricular tachycardia, to ventricular flutter, and then to a flat line.

Sudden death: the step from life into the expanse of timelessness is awesome. I'll never forget the terror in the eyes of one patient as his tenuous grasp on life loosened and he slipped into eternity. The chilling scene was burned into my memory, because I sensed he died without hope and without God.

I've also held the hand of the terminally ill and watched as the soft expression of peace replaced the taught visage of suffering as God gently led the person's spirit through the valley of the shadow of death.

From the tiny baby, to the robust athlete, I've seen the grim reaper swing his ghastly sickle, cutting down anyone in his path. As a Navy doctor, on the bloody shores of Omaha Beach, and as Chief of Emergency Medical Services in the Emergency Department of a major university medical center, the drama of making life and death decisions was a frequent occurrence. Jesus conquered death, and thwarting death is one of the most dramatic miracles one can witness. For me, there is one battle with death that stands out above all others.

When my wife, Bernice, developed multiple infarct dementia my medical training told me she had a terminal disease; one for which there's no cure. The irreversible stepwise descent to the grave was inevitable.

The first symptoms began in 1985. By 1995, she had slipped into a florid organic psychosis. Her memory was totally gone. I was a total stranger to her. Our marriage, our children, and our forty-seven happy years together were erased from her mind. Her paranoid delusions and her manic behavior gradually wore away my strength and I had to have her hospitalized. Her behavior, on the locked psychiatric ward, was so disruptive she had to be put in physical restraints.

Five days went by, and with her in the hospital I slept, ate regular meals and regained my strength. In spite of the past stress of caring for her, the longing to have her back was overwhelming. I told the doctor at the hospital that I wanted to bring her home.

"She's too ill to be taken care of at home," he said. "She's in the terminal stages of dementia and when she leaves here she should be admitted to an extended care facility for terminal care."

"I know." I said. "I'll see what I can do."

I brought her home and saw she was dying. Medication had quieted her, but she had given up the thought of living. Her shuffling gait, the blank listless stare, and the emotional withdrawal from her environment indicated to me she was ready to leave the world of terror and confusion she had struggled so long to escape.

I prayed, "Dear God, I love her so much. Please, can I have her a little longer?"

Days went by, and the stress of caring for her again began to exhaust my physical resources. But I continued to pray, "Lord give me strength."

When I thought I could go on no longer the first phase of a miracle occurred. The Caregiver, who had taken care of Bernice's father after he had a stroke, agreed to come in several hours a day and help me with her hygienic needs. The second phase of the miracle is beyond my comprehension. Bernice began to get better.

I've done research on dementia for a major drug company. In my thirty years of general medical practice, I've cared for hundreds of demented patients. I've never seen any of them make a sustained improvement. Medical literature indicates Vascular Dementia is a fatal disease with a stepwise downward course ending in death. But God's prognosis was different from that of medical science. He had a miracle in mind.

One day I opened my Bible and read: *"This sickness will not end in death. No, it is for God's glory so that God's Son may be glorified through it."* ***John 11:4***

Bernice's hospitalization occurred over seven years ago, and although her seventy-five years of life have taken their toll on her body, her mind continues to make small steps toward recovery.

I'm no longer a stranger to her. Her comprehension and orientation to her environment is markedly improved. Much of her bizarre behavior has disappeared. She hasn't been on regular medication for years and she has needed only an occasional mild tranquilizer for agitation.

Every week, lost words are being restored to her vocabulary, and our verbal and non-verbal communication continues to be enhanced. The marvelous aspect of this improvement is that many times a day she will pat me on the arm, or take my hand and tell me she loves me. The miracle that occurred in her life has occurred in mine also. The terrible specter of one of humanities most devastating diseases has turned into a miracle beyond my understanding and my faith in God's goodness has been strengthened immeasurably.

A prominent television Bible teacher insists the age of miracles is over. I wonder if he believes in answered prayer? If he does, where does he draw the line between an answered prayer and a genuine miracle? All answered prayers are miracles, whether it's Elijah calling down fire from heaven to consume the sacrifice, or one of His children saying, "Give us this day our daily bread." I can assure you the age of miracles is not over.

As a child, I lived in an atmosphere of miracles. My parents were ministers of a small church in Baltimore, Maryland. During the depression years of the early thirties, their income was frequently inadequate to meet the needs of our family. More than once we were totally without food in the house, but we were never hungry. A bag of groceries, a hot casserole, a couple of chickens or some other item appropriate to our need would show up anonymously on our doorstep.

I remember one particular time when our cupboard was bare. It was about three o'clock in the afternoon and there was nothing for dinner, not even a slice of bread.

The phone rang.

It was Mrs. Blank. She had just baked an oyster pie, and if we wanted it for dinner could someone come over and pick it up?

My brother despised Mrs. Blank. Her narrow angular face, sunken eyes, chalky complexion and graying black hair fit in with her garrulous, high pitched voice. She was always nice enough to me, but I was a cute little boy who could care less about the looks of someone who wanted to give me something delicious to eat. My brother, however, was a sophisticated teenager with a driver's license.

My mother assured Mrs. Blank someone would be right over to pick up the oyster pie.

She hung up the phone and handed the car keys to my brother." You two boys go over and get our dinner."

"I don't want to go," my brother protested. "I'd rather go hungry than to have to eat a pie she made."

"Well," my mother replied, "you can go hungry, but we're going to be eating oyster pie for dinner."

As I walked out the door, I said to my mother, "Don't worry; he'll be eating humble pie tonight."

Sometimes the answer to our prayers may come from a source we dislike. Every now and then God provides humble pie as a dietary supplement to His miraculous answers to our prayers.

Some tele-evangelists believe you can have miracles on demand. Oral Roberts in his book *A Daily Guide to Miracles* says, "I can expect a miracle every day."[1] The Foundation

---

[1] A Daily Guide to Miracles

for Inner Peace has published a two-volume set, plus a study guide, entitled *A Course in Miracles.*

The very thought of miracles fascinates people for a number of reasons. Basic psychiatry teaches that within the ego there remains a primitive longing for omnipotence, and that desire for omnipotence can best be expressed by having the power to perform miracles to satisfy one's ego desires.

In my opinion, herein lies a problem: Do we want a miracle for selfish reasons, for ego enhancement, or for a divinely approved purpose? I have the unsettling feeling that many people seeking miracles have a selfish interest in their occurrence.

The age of miracles is not over, but I think few people have an accurate understanding of miracles. Let me explain.

Miracles fall into three categories: The first and most common kind of miracle is one of Timing. To the unbeliever this is nothing more than a serendipitous confluence of events beneficial to the recipient, but to the Christian it can be a fantastic answer to prayer. Statistically, the meeting of our needs by repeated occurrences of serendipitous events, in answer to prayer, favors the conclusion they are interventions by God, rather than purely chance occurrences. The confluence of random circumstances that result in the supplying of a particular need, at a critical time, is the most frequent way God answers prayer.

In connection with this, one must be alert to recognize the answer when it comes, and to be very careful not to dictate to God the method He must use to supply your need.

A story comes to mind that illustrates this point:

A river in a Midwestern farming community began to flood. Authorities issued a flood warning and advised residents to move to high ground. A very devout farmer, whose property was in the flood zone, prayed earnestly to be spared.

The water began to rise. The sheriff drove by and called to the farmer, "There is a huge crest coming down the river; you better get out now."

"No," the farmer answered, "I've prayed and God is going to protect me."

The water rose and covered his porch. A National Guardsman came by in a boat.

"The water is going to get pretty high, get in and we'll take you to dry land."

"No," the farmer said, "God will take care of me."

The water rose to roof level and the farmer climbed up there to keep dry. Soon a helicopter flew over and called to him. "The water's still rising, we'll lower a harness and take you to safety."

"No," the farmer said, "God is going to take care of me."

The helicopter flew away and the water continued to rise. The farmer climbed up on his chimney.

A tree came floating by and got hung up on the chimney. The farmer's faith began to weaken and he thought of grabbing hold of the tree and floating away, but then he said to himself, 'No, I'm not going to doubt. I still believe God answers prayer and I'm going to stay here and trust Him.'

The water continued to rise and the farmer drowned.

He was ushered into the presence of God. "God," he said, "why did I have to drown? I've been a faithful servant of yours. Why didn't you answer my prayer?"

God looked at him in deep sympathy and said, "I did my best. I sent the sheriff, a boat, a helicopter and finally a tree to save you and you rejected every one of my efforts to rescue you."

When we pray, the miracle of an answer to prayer may take any one of many forms. Whether it's a doctor, an antibiotic, or an outright unexplained occurrence, it's God's decision which method He's going to use, not yours.

The second type of miracle is a Spiritual one, and it's even more impressive than those of timing. It's the miracle that occurs within the personality.

For twenty years, I included the sub-specialty of psychiatry in my practice of medicine. The dynamic change I've seen in a person's personality from developing a relationship with God is, in my opinion, even greater than the miracle of physical healing in answer to prayer.

An excellent example of this is the case of an alcoholic presented at Grand Rounds at Duke University when I was in Medical School. Addictive disorders are much more difficult to treat than the usual physical diseases. The goal in physical disorders is to find the proper modality of treatment for a particular disease or injury. In addictive disorders the goal is to change a deeply set mental pattern that generally is not responsive to ordinary will power.

People with physical illness usually want to get well. People with addictive disorders will say, on a superficial level of consciousness, they want to get well, but on a deeper level they cling tenaciously to their addiction. When a person with an addictive disorder is instantaneously healed through a personal relationship with Jesus Christ it's as great a miracle as the disappearance of a cancer through prayer. There should be no doubt in anyone's mind this is a true miracle.

The third type of miracle is what might be called a Cosmic miracle. The first two types of miracles involve events and forces familiar to us in our everyday lives.

The Cosmic miracle is an extremely rare event in which God uses laws and forces of nature, not available to us in everyday life, to answer a prayer request. Examples of this are events like Elijah calling down fire from heaven, Joshua's 'long day', and Jesus walking on the water. I'm not aware of any Cosmic miracles happening recently, but I believe they can happen just as easily today as they did in Biblical times. Jesus performed Cosmic miracles; e.g.: walking on the water, raising the dead and tele-transportation. The reason for their scarcity isn't because the age of miracles is past, it's because the need for them has not occurred recently. In fact, such miracles are prophesied for the 'Last Days'.

"Immediately after the distress of those days the sun will be darkened, and the moon will not give its light; the stars will fall from the sky, and the heavenly bodies will be shaken." **Matthew 24:29**

Hebrews 13:8 says, *"Jesus Christ is the same yesterday, and to day, and forever."* Since there is no passage of time with God He can do today the same miracles He did two thousand years ago, and He will do whatever is necessary to accomplish His plan for this age.

The modern skepticism about miracles is due to a lack of understanding of how modern theories of theoretical physics can be used to explain their occurrence. Even Evangelical Christians give pause to accepting Cosmic miracles.

In past chapters, we have already looked at several Cosmic miracles, and how they can be explained by scientific theories not available for use by us today. An important thing to remember is that ordinary humans have done almost all of the miracles done by Jesus. But let's look at a quick review of some of them.

Jesus fed the five thousand with a few loaves and fishes.

"We have here only five loaves of bread and two fish," they answered.

"Bring them here to me," He said *"And he directed the people to sit down on the grass. Taking the five loaves and the two fish and looking up to heaven, he gave thanks and broke the loaves. Then he gave them to the disciples, and the disciples gave them to the people. They all ate and were satisfied, and the disciples picked up twelve basketfuls of broken pieces that were left over. The number of those who ate was about five thousand men, besides women and children."* **Matthew 14:17-21**

Elijah and the widow:

Elijah said to her, *"Don't be afraid. Go home and do as you have said. But first make a small cake of bread for me from what you have and bring it to me, and then make something for yourself and your son. For this is what the LORD, the God of Israel, says: 'The jar of flour will not be used up and the jug of oil will not run dry until the day the LORD gives rain on the land.'" She went away and did as Elijah had told her. So there was food every day for Elijah and for the woman and her family. For the jar of flour was not used up and the jug of oil did not run dry, in keeping with the word of the LORD spoken by Elijah."* **1 Kings 17: 14-16**

These miracles can be easily understood in the context of the fourth dimension (Linear time-space measurement of physical objects.)

Jesus entering a room with the doors closed.

"On the evening of that first day of the week, when the disciples were together, with the doors locked for fear of the Jews, Jesus came and stood among them and said, "Peace be with you!" **John 20:19**

Paul released from prison:

"We found the jail securely locked, with the guards standing at the doors; but when we opened them, we found no one inside." **Acts 5:23**

Jesus raising Lazarus from the dead:

"Jesus had been speaking of his death, but his disciples thought he meant natural sleep. So then he told them plainly, 'Lazarus is dead.' **John 11: 13-14** *Jesus called in a loud voice, 'Lazarus, come out!' The dead man came out, his hands and feet wrapped with strips of linen, and a cloth around his face. Jesus said to them, 'Take off the grave clothes and let him go.' And he that was dead came forth, bound hand and foot with grave-clothes: and his face was bound about with a napkin. Jesus saith unto them, Loose him, and let him go."* **John 11:43-44**

Paul bringing the young man back to life:

"Seated in a window was a young man named Eutychus, who was sinking into a deep sleep as Paul talked on and on. When he was sound asleep, he fell to the ground from the third story and was picked up dead. Paul went down, threw himself on the young man and put his arms around him. 'Don't be alarmed,' He said. 'He's alive!'" **Acts 20:9-10**

This was accomplished by the reversal of time, much like running a movie film backward, except this was actually a reversal of forward movement on the time-space plane.

Teleportation: The instantaneous relocation of an object from one place to another:

"When he was at the table with them, he took bread, gave thanks, broke it and began to give it to them. Then their eyes were opened and they recognized him, and he disappeared from their sight." **Luke 24:30-31**

Philip and the Eunuch:

"When they came up out of the water, the Spirit of the Lord suddenly took Philip away, and the eunuch did not see him again, but went on his way rejoicing. Philip, however, appeared at Azotus and traveled about, preaching the gospel in all the towns until he reached Caesarea." **Acts 8:39-40**

This event is consistent with time-travel and the elimination of the passage of time.

The miracles mentioned above fall into my classification of 'cosmic' miracles. The many miracles of healing done by Jesus and the disciples are 'time' miracles.

The healing of the demonic was a spiritual miracle.

"When Jesus got out of the boat, a man with an evil spirit came from the tombs to meet him. This man lived in the tombs, and no one could bind him any more, not even with a chain. For he had often been chained hand and foot, but he tore the chains apart and broke the irons on his feet. No one was strong enough to subdue him. Night and day among the tombs and in the hills he would cry out and cut himself with stones.

When he saw Jesus from a distance, he ran and fell on his knees in front of him. He shouted at the top of his voice, "What do you want with me, Jesus, Son of the Most High God? Swear to God that you won't torture me!" For Jesus had said to him, "Come out of this man, you evil spirit!"

Then Jesus asked him, "What is your name?" "My name is Legion," he replied, "for we are many."

And he begged Jesus again and again not to send them out of the area.

A large herd of pigs was feeding on the nearby hillside. The demons begged Jesus, "Send us among the pigs; allow us to go into them."

He gave them permission, and the evil spirits came out and went into the pigs. The herd, about two thousand in number, rushed down the steep bank into the lake and were drowned. Those tending the pigs ran off and reported this in the town and countryside, and the people went out to see what had happened.

When they came to Jesus, they saw the man who had been possessed by the legion of demons, sitting there, dressed and in his right mind; and they were afraid." **Mark 5:2-15**

This was an example of a Spiritual miracle, and represents God's ability to change the past. I believe it's easier to have faith for the miracles of physical healing than it is to have faith for spiritual healing, because the subconscious resistance to change is not present.

Finally, one must always remember the phrase from the Lord's Prayer, *"Thy will be done on earth, as it is in heaven."* **Matthew 6:10** A miracle may not always be part of God's plan for the situation you're praying about. Remember the apostle Paul.

"To keep me from becoming conceited because of these surpassingly great revelations, there was given me a thorn in my flesh, a messenger of Satan, to torment me. Three times I pleaded with the Lord to take it away from me, but he said to me, "My grace is sufficient for you, for my power is made perfect in weakness. "Therefore I will boast all the more gladly about my weaknesses, so that Christ's power may rest on me. That is why, for Christ's sake, I delight in weaknesses, in insults, in hardships, in persecutions, in difficulties. For when I am weak, then I am strong." **2 Corinthians 12:7-10**

Chapter Twelve
Past Perfect — Future Perfect

Are you a perfect Christian? If not, you're not a Christian at all. Frightening isn't it?

Jesus said, *"Be perfect, therefore, as your heavenly Father is perfect."* **Matthew 5:48** *"But if we claim to be without sin, we deceive ourselves and the truth is not in us."* **1 John 1:8** We will discuss this paradox a little later, but in the meantime we must be sure we have complied with the conditions necessary for our salvation.

There are three things that must occur in order for a person to become a perfect Christian. None of these three things standing alone can accomplish our eternal salvation. While all three elements are essential, the third event is the one that gives us the stamp of God's assurance that we are saved.

The first of these three events is intellectual assent. You have to know what it is you believe and accept the validity of that belief before it can become real to you.

"Believe in the Lord Jesus, and you will be saved." **Acts 16:31**

The second event is a physical expression of that belief to others. *"For it is with your heart that you believe and are justified, and it is with your mouth that you confess and are saved."* **Romans 10:10**

The third event is a personality change from being ego-centric to being God centered. This is accomplished when we ask God for His forgiveness and keep the great commandment.

One of the teachers of the law — asked him, *"Of all the commandments, which is the most important?"*

"The most important one," answered Jesus, *"is this: 'Hear, O Israel, the Lord our God, the Lord is one. Love the*

Lord your God with all your heart and with all your soul and with all your mind and with all your strength.' The second is this: 'Love your neighbor as yourself. There is no commandment greater than these.'" **Mark 12:28-31**

The most essential part of this personality change is forgiving those who have wronged us. *"Forgive us the wrong we have done and then **we [must] forgive others who have wronged us**."* **Matthew 6:12**

Forgiving others who have wronged us is contrary to a basic psychological instinct. The natural psychological reaction is to hate, escape [from the threatening environment] retaliate and/or negotiate. Jesus said, *"You have heard that it was said, 'Love your neighbor and hate your enemy. But I tell you: Love your enemies and pray for those who persecute you, **that you may be sons of your Father in heaven**.'"* **Matthew 5:44**

First of all, we must keep in mind there is absolutely nothing we can do to be saved. Our salvation is a free unmerited gift from God. The common misconception is that if a person believes Jesus is the Son of God and died for our sins he will be saved. The basis for this misconception (that this is all one has to do to be saved) is found in **Acts 16:31**. *"Believe on the Lord Jesus Christ and thou shalt be saved."* But believing is not enough. *"You believe that there is one God. Good! Even the demons believe that—and shudder.* **James 2:19** *"Two demon-possessed men coming from the tombs met him. They were so violent that no one could pass that way. "What do you want with us, Son of God?" they shouted. "Have you come here to torture us before the appointed time?"* **Matthew 8:28-29**

There is no doubt Scripture demonstrates the devil recognized, Jesus as the Son of God, and was fully aware of why He had come to earth. **Matthew 4:1-11** clearly states Satan believed who Jesus claimed to be. However, believing in the deity of Jesus and that He redeemed us from the bondage of sin, by His death and resurrection is only the first of the three events needed for salvation.

The second event is that we verbally testify to the reality of our faith. *"That if you confess with your mouth, "Jesus is Lord," and believe in your heart that God raised him from the dead, you will be saved."* **Romans 10:9** The demons mentioned in **Matthew 8:28-29** confessed that Jesus was the Son of God and I'm sure they believed in their heart that God would raise Him from the dead; yet this alone was not enough.

Even good works done in the name of Jesus, along with believing and confession of faith in Christ, is not enough.

"Many will say to me on that day, 'Lord, Lord, did we not prophesy in your name, and in your name drive out demons and perform many miracles? 'Then I will tell them plainly, 'I never knew you. Away from me, you evildoers." **Matthew 7:22-23**

These people believed in Jesus and they confessed with their mouth that He was Lord, and even cast out demons in His name, yet they were not saved. The reason they were not saved is that they were not perfect. Another factor was needed for their salvation. This brings us to the third event that needs to occur in our lives before we are saved.

The occurrence of this event indicates we have become perfect in the eyes of God. When we reach this state of perfection it doesn't mean we no longer sin. Paul tells us that.

"Not that I have already obtained all this, or have already been made perfect, but I press on to take hold of that for which Christ Jesus took hold of me." **Philippians 3:12**

We continue to struggle as Paul did, with our sinful nature as described in **Romans** chapter **7** and **8**, *"I do not understand what I do. For what I want to do I do not do, but what I hate I do."* **Romans 7:15** and **19** *"For what I do is not the good I want to do; no, the evil I do not want to do I keep on doing."* Yet he goes on to say. *"Therefore, there is now **no condemnation** for those who are in Christ Jesus."* **Romans 8:1** In spite of our continuing to sin, the Bible tells us to be perfect. *"Be **perfect**, therefore, as your heavenly Father is perfect."* **Matthew 5: 43-48** *"Because by one sacrifice he has **made perfect forever those who are being made holy**."* **Hebrews 10:14**

The answer to why we are perfect is really very simple. First, from the Biblical standpoint, the above verse in Hebrews gives us a hint; *we are being made perfect* (holy); not by anything we can do, have done, or will do, but because we have totally committed our lives to God so He can make us perfect. *"Who has saved us and called us to a holy life—not because of anything we have done but because of his own purpose and grace. This grace was given us in Christ Jesus before the beginning of time." 2 Timothy 1:9*

We accept the above verses by faith, not always realizing that God has provided a rational explanation of how His Grace works, both from Scripture and from science. The Bible says God is not bound by time. *"I am Alpha and Omega, the beginning and the ending, saith the Lord, which is, and which was, and which is to come, the Almighty." Revelation 1:8 "the darkness and the light are both alike to thee." Psalms 139:12* In *Exodus 3:14 "God said to Moses, "I AM WHO I AM. This is what you are to say to the Israelites: 'I AM has sent me to you.'"* In other words, God was saying He is not a God of the past or of the future; He is a God of "NOW", always in the eternal present.

This impacts on our idea of forgiveness in a remarkable way. It implies that when we ask for forgiveness God not only looks at our past sins, or the sins we are presently committing, He also sees the sins we are going to commit (in fact, these sins have already been committed in the future, but we are not aware of them yet).

The linchpin of this argument is that salvation cannot occur until we forgive those who have sinned against us, and our carnal nature rebels against this command. When we are born again our new nature supplants the selfish, defensive nature with which we were born. Therefore, when He forgives our sins (after we have forgiven those who have sinned against us) He has forgiven all our sins, past, present, and future and we're perfect in His Eyes by virtue of the pardon purchased for us on Calvary. It's not that the physical event of sinning has changed, it's because a new motive for not wanting to sin has developed. I believe the spirit of mankind is timeless and when God makes us a new creature in Christ Jesus He changes our motive from living for the pursuit of sin to a quest for righteousness.

But in order for this to happen, we must be sure to comply with the third condition for salvation mentioned above. We must forgive those who have sinned against us. In the parable of the unjust servant Jesus explains the importance of this to Peter.

"Then Peter came to Jesus and asked, "Lord, how many times shall I forgive my brother when he sins against me? Up to seven times?"

Jesus answered, "I tell you, not seven times, but seventy-seven times.

"Therefore, the kingdom of heaven is like a king who wanted to settle accounts with his servants. As he began the settlement, a man who owed him ten thousand talents was brought to him. Since he was not able to pay, the master ordered that he and his wife and his children and all that he had be sold to repay the debt.

"The servant fell on his knees before him. 'Be patient with me,' he begged, 'and I will pay back everything.'

The servant's master took pity on him, canceled the debt and let him go. "But when that servant went out, he found one of his fellow servants who owed him a hundred denarii. He grabbed him and began to choke him. 'Pay back what you owe me!' he demanded. his fellow servant fell to his knees and begged him, 'Be patient with me, and I will pay you back.'

"But he refused. Instead, he went off and had the man thrown into prison until he could pay the debt.

When the other servants saw what had happened, they were greatly distressed and went and told their master everything that had happened. Then the master called the servant in. 'You wicked servant,' he said, 'I canceled all that debt of yours because you begged me to shouldn't you have had mercy on your fellow servant just as I had on you?'

In anger his master turned him over to the jailers to be tortured, until he should pay back all he owed. 'This is how my heavenly Father will treat each of you unless you forgive your brother from your heart.'"

"For the would-be Christian there is no other parable more frightening than this one. The thing so terrible about this lesson is that sometimes it seems like an impossible task to forgive some of the things that have been done to us. It is only by completely surrendering the integrity of one's personality and the independence of the will to God that this can be accomplished.

One can derive a deeper understanding of forgiveness from this parable, other than just the forgiveness of individual sins. Jesus was telling Peter, that it's not the number of sins committed against you that's important; it involves a change in your attitude toward the sinner. If you expect God to forgive your sins, there must be a change in your attitude toward your debtor.

Forgiveness then becomes an attitude of love, not just an intellectual act, and like God's forgiveness of your sins past, present, and future, you must forgive not only those who have already sinned against you, but also those who will sin against you in the future; no matter how grievous or how many times they do it, or will do it. In other words, *"Love your enemies, bless them that curse you, do good to them that hate you, and pray for them which despitefully use you, and persecute you."* **Matthew 5:44** When we earnestly strive to do this as part of our new spiritual nature, it's evidence that the redemptive process has occurred in our hearts.

When we comply with these three requirements, God removes our sins as if they had never occurred.

"I have swept away your offenses like a cloud, your sins like the morning mist." **Isaiah 44:22** If my sins are separated from me, " *as far as the east is from the west, so far has he removed our transgressions from us."* **Psalms 103:12** *"He will have compassion upon us; he will subdue our iniquities; and thou wilt cast all their sins into the depths of the sea."* **Micah 7:19** Then I'm no longer guilty of sin in God's eyes, and I'm perfect. *"Be ye therefore perfect,*

even as your Father which is in heaven is perfect."
Matthew 5:48

If I'm forgiven and no longer accountable for my sins why do I feel such remorse?

When your sins are forgiven you no longer need to feel guilt. Guilt is destructive, Judas felt tremendous guilt for betraying Jesus and he went out and hanged himself. He also felt remorse, but it was too late to do any good. It's from guilt that you're redeemed. Remorse is appropriate and constructive.

Peter suffered tremendous remorse when he denied he knew Jesus. Peter remembered that event the rest of his life and never denied he knew Jesus again. In fact, he died rather than be disloyal to his Lord and master. Remorse teaches righteousness; it reminds us of our need for a closer walk with Jesus. The greater our remorse the more diligently we depend on the wisdom, strength and compassion of our Lord.

I've listened to hundreds of ministers give marvelous sermons on salvation, and I've seen thousands of penitents come forward at alter calls. But I remember few instances of any minister telling them that a consequence of their decision, to accept Jesus Christ as their Savior, is a desire to tell others of their new Faith and experience the joy of forgiving those who have sinned against them.

The hurt, the pain, the bitterness, the disappointment, the anger, the desire for revenge caused by the acts of others toward you must go in order for you to experience the wonderful gift of love expressed by God in our salvation.

There is no forgiveness for us until we have forgiven all those who have sinned against us. It's when the animosity towards others, who have sinned against us, disappears as the morning mist that we become perfect and our salvation is finalized for all eternity.

When you offer forgiveness it can not be an intellectual exercise it must come from the heart. A true offer of forgiveness entails a compassion for the one who has sinned against you and you must act accordingly.

Don't expect to forget the grievance against you; that can be a virtual impossibility. You must go back to that event in the long body of your past and forgive the person while the grievance is still actually being committed. When one becomes a Christian the new person that comes into being does not start on the day salvation is recognized; it is a total change (new birth) in your entire 'long body' life span from beginning to end.

The fact you are obligated by God to offer forgiveness to those who have sinned against you in order for your salvation to be complete does not mean the persons who sinned against you is forgiven by God. Their sin is not forgiven until they are born again. The only thing you can, and must do is to offer forgiveness regardless whether you are asked for forgiveness or not. Jesus offered Judas forgiveness when He washed the disciples feet, but it was not accepted. He offered forgiveness to those who were crucifying Him. Jesus said, *"Father, forgive them, for they do not know what they are doing." Luke 23:34* The willingness to forgive from the heart is an important element of Salvation.

When you offer forgiveness it can not be an intellectual exercise it must come from the heart. A true offer of forgiveness entails a compassion for the one who has sinned against you and you must act accordingly.

✦   ✦   ✦   ✦   ✦

Do you remember the first time you consciously sinned? I do. I was only five years old. I sinned deliberately, with a full awareness of what I was doing. It was 1919 and our family lived in an apartment on Macon Street in Brooklyn, New York. My sister was ten years older than I, and we were brought up to honor God by tithing the money we either earned, or was given to us. She kept her tithe in a little tin box in a drawer in her bedroom.

One day I stepped on that famous "slippery slope" when I went into her room and started investigating what she had in her bureau. The little tin box had an alluring jingle. With much tugging and twisting I removed the lid, and there before me was a bunch of pennies and a few nickels. We were poor, and pennies could buy candy, and a nickel translated into a toy or a bottle of pop. The little green demons of covetousness and greed tempted me to put my hand in the box and take just one nickel and a few pennies not enough to be missed, but plenty to satisfy my selfishness.

I felt guilty, but did I put the money back? No, I devised a plan to explain where I got the money. I took my newfound wealth outside and looking up and down the street to make sure no one was coming, I carefully put it down on a ledge of our apartment building next to the sidewalk. I walked a short distance down the sidewalk, turned around and came back to where I had placed the money. 'Oh', I said to myself, 'look what I've found.' I gathered up the money, went running into the house and said, "Mother, look what I found on that little ledge of our apartment next to the sidewalk."

"That's wonderful," she replied as she counted out the nine cents I showed her. "Now be sure you put a penny into the tithe."

I told my sister the same story when she came home. She didn't miss the money, or at least didn't mention it.

I never forgot what I did and it continued to trouble me. Six years later, at the age of eleven, I confessed my misdeed to my sister and offered to pay her back with substantial interest. By then she was twenty-one and quite amused by the story. She didn't want the money back, but I kept insisting. Finally she realized this was part of my penance, so she took the money and put it in the collection plate the next Sunday.

That was the first of my many sins of commission I remember. It was followed by many sins of omission. These were terrible experiences that make me cringe as I look back on them. An example occurred the first day I wore my naval uniform in public.

The Pennsylvania Railway Station in Philadelphia was bustling with people rushing to get on trains, rushing to get off trains, and rushing to get a taxi to take them to some place where the same frenetic pace would continue. It was May of 1943, and I'd just been ordered to active duty in the Navy.

Wearing a dark blue uniform bearing one and a half gold stripes on the sleeve, a white shirt, black tie and a white navy cap with the gold insignia on the front, I was a stranger to myself, as well as to the hundreds of people milling around the station.

While I waited for my train to be called, an attractive well-dressed young girl came running up to the Travelers Aid desk near where I was standing. She was panicked. Through sobs and tears she explained to the desk attendant, "I thought I had a job in Philadelphia, but it's been filled, and I'm without funds to get home."

The woman at the Travelers Aid said, "I'm sorry, but we don't have any money to give travelers. We only give advice."

"But can't you give me enough money to phone a friend who might help me?"

"No, I'm sorry we can't even do that."

I felt conspicuous and uncomfortable in my new uniform, but my heart melted within me. How could I help this poor girl?

It didn't seem proper for a naval officer to go up to a strange woman in a public place and offer her money. I thought of giving it to the Traveler Aid attendant and have her give it to the desperate woman, but that wouldn't work because she was standing right there and would know what was happening. While I wrestled with this dilemma, my train was called and I had to leave. Fifty-eight years later, I'm still suffering from my failure to act. Since then I have thought of a dozen ways I could have handled the situation. The haunting expressions on that girl's face and the terror of abandonment in her voice are as real today as if the event were yesterday. When I think of her, I think of the words of Jesus:

"For I was hungry and you gave me nothing to eat, I was thirsty and you gave me nothing to drink, was a stranger and you did not invite me in, I needed clothes and you did not clothe me, I was sick and in prison and you did not look after me.'

"They also will answer, 'Lord, when did we see you hungry or thirsty or a stranger or needing clothes or sick or in prison, and did not help you?'

"He will reply, 'I tell you the truth, whatever you did not do for one of the least of these, you did not do for me.'

"Then they will go away to eternal punishment, but the righteous to eternal life." **Matthew 25: 42-46**

What sins of commission or omission are haunting you? There are many in my life; in fact, the sins of omission concern me more than the sins of commission. This is not because my failure to act is worse than the sins I have actually committed. My sins of omission and commission have all been forgiven. They're not there anymore. They've been separated from me "as far as the East is from the West." It's the lessons I've learned and the remorse I've felt from those failures that are so deeply burned into my mind. With the help of God, I'll never neglect the opportunity to help another person in such drastic need.

It's important that we consider the sins we know are forgiven in the light of science as well as in theology. Let's discuss the scientific reasons first. These may surprise you.

The scientific implications of this are disturbing. Every sin you've ever committed, every mistake you've ever made is still being committed, according to an accepted scientific theory. Once an act is done, you can do nothing to change it. It becomes part of your frozen past, just as real to you, to others and to God, as the moment you did it. Every harsh word is still being spoken, every selfish act is still being carried out, every lustful thought is still in your mind. This is not a philosophical illusion of mine. Let me repeat what Dr. Fred Allen Wolf, a secular theoretical physicist said. "Your whole life history lies (*on the time-space plane*)[italics mine] like a gigantic centipede stuck in plastic —All your ups and downs are just frozen wiggles in the worm." [1]

Furthermore, on the Day of Judgment, the sins of the unsaved, past, present and future (future sins are already there) will be visible to everyone. They're all exposed to

---

[1] Parallel Universes, P.120

public view, and they're a permanent part of their eternal body. The Biblical affirmation of this is found *in Luke 12: 2* and *3 "There is nothing concealed that will not be disclosed, or hidden that will not be made known. What you have said in the dark will be heard in the daylight, and what you have whispered in the ear in the inner rooms will be proclaimed from the roofs."*

This is scientifically accurate. Einstein says, "World lines (*the things that have occurred in the past*) are an accepted concept of relativity and can't be changed, altering the past is not possible in relativity."[2] No human can alter the past or the future. One can easily understand why the past can't be altered, but it's more difficult for us to understand that the future can't be altered.

Why can't a person decide what he or she wants to do from minute to minute, day by day? The reason is because there is no difference between past and future; they're undifferentiated and everything you're going to do is seen as an eternal "NOW," on our time-space plane. Your innate will has already decided how you will react in every future situation.

In an eternity of higher dimensions, the unsaved will be seen as the frozen centipede that Dr. Wolf uses as an illustration. The person will be an intact physical object from the time he was identified as that person until a period in future time when his personal identity is lost. In other words, material things, including people, have no past or future, just a fourth dimension on a time plane called "NOW," where past, present and future are all present at once.

If everything we'll experience in the future is already there, and it's just as unchangeable as the past, then why should we even try to change our behavior?

Because, when we become Christians, we are freed from the shackles of time, *"Jesus replied, "I tell you the truth, everyone who sins is a slave to sin. So if the Son sets you free, you will be free indeed." **John 8:3,36** **The shackles of time are a consequence of sin and time is the sentence of death**. The non-Christian is stuck with a fatalistic future, but for the

---

[2] Hyperspace p 238

Christian God changes world lines. Our free will can again operate to be obedient to God and earn rewards in heaven.

When God accepts us and forgives our sins, we become free from the bondage of time. Not only the past is gone but also the sins, the failures, the hate and anger that we may experience in the future is also gone in the eyes of God if we have been truly born again. We will have our free will back and we're again free to make decisions. Our obedience to God is now voluntary, and He can use our free will to further His kingdom. The world and all humanity are prisoners of time, bound by sin, but those who become Christians are free and can be instruments of God to bring others to the realization they may also be free.

Once forgiven, we should not look back at the sinful life of the past. Remember Lott's wife who became immobilized when she secretly longed for the comforts, the luxuries, the pleasures and the security she was leaving, instead of looking forward to the Promised Land to which she was going. It's a struggle to leave the pleasures of the world behind and not to think of resisted temptations as lost opportunities, but God has something much better for us, and that something will last forever.

Even after knowing all this, we tend to feel guilt and think of our past sins and failures in a negative context. When we are harassed by our past failures, we should remember our sins are forgiven and no longer imputed to our account. *"But if we walk in the light, as he is in the light, we have fellowship with one another, and the blood of Jesus, his Son, purifies us from all sin."* **1 John 1:7**

We still feel remorse but we no longer need to feel guilt, and when feelings of guilt persist, remember what Paul says about such thoughts,

"We demolish arguments and every pretension that sets itself up against the knowledge of God, and we take captive every thought to make it obedient to Christ." **2 Corinthians 10:5**

Once forgiven, our past as well as our future is now perfect, not by anything we have done, but by the blood of Christ and the grace of God.

What a wonderful opportunity we have. No other religion or philosophy has proposed such a wonderful option. Science isn't going to help; it was science that made us aware of our deplorable state of bondage to sin. Trying to be good, to be a better person, a more productive citizen, will not prevent the sins of the future, or remedy the sins of the past, because according to scientific theory those world lines can't be changed, but God can forgive our sins and change our lives. And changing lives is what Christianity is all about.

When I was in medical school at Duke University, I witnessed a powerful example of a life that was enslaved by time and one that was liberated by the power of God's forgiveness. This was demonstrated at Psychiatric Grand Rounds.

At Grand Rounds a professor selects a clinical problem and then presents patients representing that problem to a gathering of faculty and medical students. Someone unfamiliar with the patient is then asked to take a history, examine the patient, make a diagnosis, and suggest appropriate treatment.

Briefly the story went somewhat like this. There were two patients. The first one we'll call Mr. Shaker; the second one, Mr. Wright. Both had a long history of alcohol abuse. Mr. Shaker was an upper-class social drinker whose health and happiness had dissolved in alcohol. When presented at Grand Rounds, he was extremely nervous, he had the shakes, his face was puffy and his eyes bloodshot and bleary.

Mr. Wright had the history of a typical bum. His rap sheet listed thirty-eight arrests in the previous year for public drunkenness, petty theft and disturbing the peace. A peace officer testified the patient had been picked up innumerable times, in an alcoholic stupor, and taken to the "drunk tank." Since his first arrest for drunkenness twelve years before, he had never been seen sober by the authorities. About three months prior to his appearance at Grand Rounds the authorities had lost track of him.

When the witnessing officer was told that Mr. Wright was one of the two patients, he didn't believe it. The "bum" was clean-shaven and neatly dressed. He had a sparkle in his eye, an infectious smile and a spring in his step. He was one of the happiest people I have ever seen.

The attention of the faculty and students was riveted on the professor presenting the cases. What magical treatment had the professor come up with to work such a dramatic cure, and could he work the same miracle in the other patient?

The professor addressed the audience. " This is a most unusual case, and because of the remarkable outcome I would like Mr. Wright to tell you about his recovery from acute and chronic alcoholism.

Mr. Wright went to the podium. "Well," he said, "I ain't much for speakin' in public, but I'm glad to tell you what happened."

"One night, when I was soused to the gills as usual, I passed the Salvation Army Mission. It was a real cold night and so I went into the mission to get warm. I don't re-member much of what the talk was about, but at the end the speaker said, 'You know, you don't have to be on the street, cold and hungry, Jesus can make you a new person. He can clean up your life and give you something worthwhile to live for. If you would like to be born again and start a new life from scratch, get out of your seat, come down here and kneel at the altar. If you believe that God loves you so much that He sent Jesus, His Son, to die for you and to cleanse you from all your sins He'll free you from the habits that have been holding you down and set you free.'"

"Well I hadn't nothin' to lose, 'ceptin' my worthless soul if'n I didn't do it, so I went down and knelt at the altar. That's the last I remember until I woke up to the smell of bacon and coffee. I was on a cot in a room with several other men. I had a pounding headache and a bad taste in my mouth, but for the first time in as long as I can remember, I had no desire for a drink. In fact, it made me sick at the stomach just to think about it."

" I was pretty shaky for several days, but the craving for alcohol is gone and I haven't had a drink since. I work at the mission now tryin' to help others with the same problem I had."

The professor said, "You can't argue with success and so we have brought Mr. Wright here to talk to Mr. Shaker and see if the same remarkable change will occur in his life."

At the close of Grand Rounds, I went up to Mr. Shaker and asked, " Do you think Mr. Wright's program will work for you?"

He shook his head and said, "No, that's not for me."

One could not have had a more dramatic example of a person being released from a future of sorrow, sickness and death, and another person, in similar circumstances, who refused to exercise his will to accept salvation and the incomprehensible love of Jesus Christ who wanted to save him from the destruction of his addiction.

Only Christianity provides a way of undoing the pain, the suffering and the sorrow of both the past and the future, of totally wiping out those imperfections and giving us a new hyperdimensional body, not just in memory but in fact. Jesus Christ paid the ransom to free us from the shackles of time. His blood wiped out the world lines that held us in bondage. Believe in the atonement of Jesus Christ, ask God's forgiveness for your sins, forgive those who have sinned against you and make your life, past and your future, perfect.

Don't look back as Lot's wife did; look ahead to the Promised Land. *"While we wait for the blessed hope—the glorious appearing of our great God and Savior, Jesus Christ, who gave himself for us to redeem us from all wickedness and to purify for himself a people that are his very own, eager to do what is good."* **Titus 2:13 and 14** *"Because by one sacrifice he has made perfect forever those who are being made holy."* **Hebrews 10:14**

Chapter Thirteen
Redefining Death

"Tomorrow and tomorrow and tomorrow creeps in this petty pace from day to day to the last syllable of recorded time, and all our yesterdays have lighted fools the way to dusty death. Out, out brief candle, life's but a fleeting shadow, a poor player who frets and struts his hour upon the stage and then is heard no more. It is a tale told by an idiot, full of sound and fury, signifying nothing."
William Shakespeare *(Macbeth)*

Woody Allen said, *"I don't mind dying; I just don't want to be there when it happens."*

The Bible says, *"And as it is appointed unto men once to die, but after this the judgment."* **Hebrews 9:27**

Death has many faces and I've seen them all. From the blue-gray pallor of a dead infant to the stony fixed gaze in the sunken eye sockets of the elderly. I've seen terror in the eyes of those who were unprepared as they drew their last breath, and I've watched the gentle passing of the terminally ill. I've fought with a passion to hold on to a thread of life in the prematurely stricken, and I've eased the suffering of those whose hope of life was gone, as they escaped from the prison of pain into the peaceful arms of death.

"Where, O death, is your victory? Where, O death, is your sting? The sting of death is sin." **1 Corinthians 15: 55-56**

What is that magic element we call life, and what happens when it leaves the flesh that's housed it? Let's explore those questions both in the context of conventional thinking and within the framework of hyperdimensional theory. First, let's look at some Bible verses about death.

"But if it is preached that Christ has been raised from the dead, how can some of you say that there is no resurrection of the dead?" **Romans 5:12**

"For since death came through a man, the resurrection of the dead comes also through a man. For as in Adam all die, so in Christ all will be made alive." **1 Corinthians 15:21-22**

"Who delivered us from so great a death, and doth deliver: in whom we trust that he will yet deliver us." **2 Corinthians 1:10**

"For since death came through a man, the resurrection of the dead comes also through a man. For as in Adam all die, so in Christ all will be made alive." **1 Corinthians 15:21**

"Jesus Our Savior Christ, who hath abolished death, and hath brought life and immortality to light through the gospel." **2 Timothy 1:10**

We may have an intellectual understanding of death, but do we have the passionate understanding; that awesome awareness of what Jesus and His friends and family suffered when He tasted death for all humanity? Let's look more closely at the picture.

✦   ✦   ✦   ✦   ✦

Her body shook with sobs. How could her life of ecstatic joy be turned into such bitter sorrow? Her memories of the past thirty-three years were as vivid as if they were yesterday.

The wonderful adventure of giving birth in a stable was eclipsed by the horror of the blood-streaked body of her son hanging on the cross. He was supposed to be a King, the Messiah, the rescuer of the Jewish nation. The shepherds had come to see Him, and angels heralded His birth.

Important sages from far away had brought Him gifts and bowed in adoration. Why did He have to die this way? He had power over death, He had raised the widow's son **Luke 7:11-15** and even though Lazarus had been dead four days, He brought him back to life. **John 11:43-44** It was only last week the crowds had proclaimed Him king; then they had turned on Him and called for His death.

She turned to the others, "This day of infamy will be remembered forever." The blackness that blotted out the sun was a reflection of the despair she felt in her heart.

"Look, He is moving," one of them, said.

Streaks of lightning flashed across the sky, the earth convulsed with a shuddering roar, and over those terrifying sounds of nature floated a blood curdling scream, *"My God, My God, why hast thou forsaken me?"* An eerie silence settled over the landscape; then, through the darkness, came the tortured words, *"It is finished."* *"At that moment the earth shook and the rocks split and in the Temple the curtain that separated the Holy Place from the Most Holy Place was torn in two from top to bottom."* **Matthew 27:51-53**

The soldier stationed at the foot of the cross looked up in reverent awe. *"Surely this man was the Son of God."* **Mark 15: 38**

The captain of the guard came by. "Break the criminal's legs. The Jewish authorities don't want them hanging on crosses on their religious holidays which begin at sunset."

The soldier standing at the foot of Jesus' cross said, "But sir, this man is already dead."

"Well, run a spear into his heart just to make sure."

The soldier took his spear and placing it just below the ribs, shoved it into the flesh, through the liver, the diaphragm and into the heart. He was dead all right, clotted blood and serum flowed from the wound. He had seen this in battle. Soldiers who had died under great stress had the same thing happen to them. Their blood clotted and separated from the serum, they called it an agonal clot. You can't live when that happens. "What a tragedy that He had to die. This has been a bad day." He said reflectively.

Joseph of Arimathea and Nicodemus (they were secret followers of Jesus,) were watching from a distance. When they saw that Jesus had died, they went to Pilate and asked for His body. Pilate gave his permission, and so they went and took the body down from the cross. The stiffness of death had already set in which made it hard for them as they wrapped His body in strips of linen. Then, they took the body and placed it in Joseph's tomb, a cave recently hewed from solid rock. Then they took a huge stone, cut into the shape of a wheel, and rolled it across the entrance.

"The next day, the one after Preparation Day, the chief priests and the Pharisees went to Pilate. "Sir," they said, "we remember that while he was still alive that deceiver said, 'After three days I will rise again So give the order for the tomb to be made secure until the third day. Otherwise, his disciples may come and steal the body and tell the people that he has been raised from the dead. This last deception will be worse than the first."

"Take a guard," Pilate answered. "Go, make the tomb as secure as you know how."

So they went and made the tomb secure by putting a seal on the stone and posting the guard. **Matthew 27:62-66**

The Disciples were devastated. They had lost their leader. In their bitter disappointment and sorrow, they completely forgot that Jesus had predicted His crucifixion and on the third day He would break the bonds of death and live again. Maybe in spirit, perhaps at the end of the age, but now He was as dead as anyone could be. No longer could they bask in the aura of His popularity. The crowds would not follow them. It was back to the boats and the fishnets.

The next day passed and on the third day, after the Sabbath, at dawn, on the first day of the week, Mary Magdalene and the other Mary went to look at the tomb. There was a violent earthquake and an angel came down from heaven (Through a wormhole?) and, going to the tomb, physically rolled back the stone and sat on it. His appearance was like lightning, and his clothes were white as snow. He scared the guards stiff; they were so afraid of him that they shook and became like dead men.

The angel said to the women, "Do not be afraid, for I know you are looking for Jesus, who was crucified. He is not here, He has risen, just as He said. Come and see the place where He lay. Then go quickly and tell His Disciples, 'He has risen from the dead and is going ahead of you into Galilee. There you will see Him. "Now I have told you."

So the women hurried away from the tomb, afraid, yet filled with joy, and ran to tell His Disciples. Suddenly Jesus met them. "Greetings," He said. They came to Him, clasped His feet and worshiped Him.

Then, Jesus said to them, "Do not be afraid. Go and tell my brothers to go to Galilee, there they will see me."

While the women were on their way, some of the guards went into the city and reported to the chief priests everything that had happened.

"On the evening of that first day of the week, when the Disciples were together, with the doors locked for fear of the Jews, Jesus came and stood among them and said, 'Peace be with you!' After he said this, he showed them his hands and side. The Disciples were overjoyed when they saw the Lord." **John 20:19**

✦   ✦   ✦   ✦   ✦

The above story, primarily from the Gospel of Matthew, illustrates a number of examples of hyperdimensional reality. The first one is the correlation of events in our five dimensional world with the reaction to these events in the realm of higher dimensions. The supernatural manifestations in nature: earthquakes, an eclipse of the sun, lightning and thunder, have reflected the power of God reacting to the catastrophic evil of mankind that has necessitated such an enormous remedy. In past chapters, we have talked about the physical resurrection of the dead and the miracles of Jesus raising some individuals from death, but, in this account, it was reported that the graves were opened; and many bodies of the saints which slept arose, and came out of the graves after his resurrection, and went into the holy city, and appeared unto many. See *Matthew 27:52,23*

The opening of graves and the dead walking about in the streets of Jerusalem is a reasonable occurrence in the light of the latest scientific theories of 'time'. Angels appearing at the time of the resurrection is another example of the interdimensional travel of hyperdimensional beings, and Jesus entering a room with all the doors closed is consistent with the latest theories of hyperspace.

Many scientists are willing to accept the concept that a basketball can be turned inside out without breaking its cover, but ridicule Christians for believing that Jesus, a man with hyperdimensional understanding and power, could do the things He did. Even though these things were in strict accordance with the theories the scientists themselves developed.

The Bible story indicates that those who came out of their graves and walked around the streets of Jerusalem did so in their recognizable natural bodies. In order for them to do so, the graves had to be opened. If they were just spirits, the graves could have remained intact.

The skeptic laughs at Christians who believe this account. How could this happen? Some of those people must have been dead for years and were no more than skeletons.

According to conventional thinking the skeptic is right, but in the light of modern theoretical physics and Christian hyperdimensional theology the event is plausible. The lives of those people who came out of their graves just had their time-space videotape run backwards. In the long body concept, they were intact in the past and just as real as the people who saw them.

To me this account substantiates my assumption that those whose life has ended are just as real and alive, on the time-space plane of the past, as those who are living in the present.

Now let's look at what happens when a person passes into the time-space world of eternity.

Bob is a very close friend and his story gives a hint of the answer; a story that is remarkably similar to hundreds of other accounts collected by physicians and psychologists who have researched this field. Here's what he told me.

"A co-worker and I were on our way back to our office following a business lunch. My co-worker was a paraplegic and he was driving his specially equipped van. I was tired and so I got in the back seat and dozed off. In retrospect, I remember a sleight jolt. The next thing I remember, I was floating above the van. It had hit a tree. It seemed I was about twenty feet above the accident, but I could see the curb by the van in minute detail, as though I was looking through a magnifying glass; the texture of the concrete with its tiny hairline cracks appeared only inches away. I had a tremendous feeling of euphoria, and, as the scene of the accident faded, I was enveloped in a brilliant radiance. Even though the light was brighter than looking directly at the noonday sun, it didn't hurt my eyes. But the most striking thing was the feeling I was out of my body; I felt weightless and free. I seemed to be in a timeless environment, and I had this feeling of peace. I didn't want to lose that feeling of absolute peace."

Bob's story is almost identical to some of those found in the book *Life After Life* by **Raymond A, Moody, M.D.** and a companion book, *Recollections of Death* by **Michael A. Sabon, M.D.** .

In the two books mentioned above, there is a remarkable consistency between the stories of 266 people who had near death experiences (NDE). Dr. Sabon has done an excellent job in portraying the phenomenon.

First, he established criteria for evidence of clinical death in the cases reported in his study. He reports, in detail, the experiences as related by his subjects and then he critiques the stories from the point of a scientific observer. He also discusses the explanations of the experiences as put forth by disbelievers in a conscious awareness of reality after a person's death.

The criticisms cover the following explanations:
1) The person was in a semi-conscious state.
2) The experience was a conscious fabrication.
3) The occurrence was a sub-conscious fabrication.
4) The extra corporal (out of the body) feeling was a result of depersonalization (a condition that occurs when the nervous system attempts to hold a potentially disorganizing emotion in check)
5) The event was a dream.

6) The experience was fabricated because of a prior expectation.
7) The event was caused by a drug induced delusion or hallucination.
8) The person undergoes a temporal lobe (brain) seizure.
9) The experience is due to an altered state of consciousness such as experienced with hallucinogens.
10) The most common explanation given was that there is a tremendous release of endorphins (a chemical in the brain associate with a feeling of euphoria.)

The question is really moot. When there are ten professional opinions involving ten possible explanations, and perhaps many more that haven't been mentioned, it indicates science has no definitive answer to the question.

When confronted by the publicity of Dr. Sabon's book, the medical community responded by publishing an article in the Journal of the American Medical Association stating that "—people who undergo these 'death experiences' are suffering from a hypoxic (lack of oxygen) state during which they try to deal —with anxieties provoked by medical procedures —We are dealing here with fantasy death. For this reason—the physician must be especially wary of accepting *religious belief* as scientific data." Dr. Sabon's response " — equal caution should be exercised in accepting *scientific belief* for scientific data.[1] From the data given by Dr. Sabon, I believe the preponderance of evidence favors the reality of NDE rather than any of the other explanations given.

In previous chapters, I have tried to explain the theoretical experiences one might have in a hyperdimensional state. So let's compare what is experienced in a NDE with what I would anticipate would be the case in an escape from our three dimensional bodies.

The following is a description of feelings and events given by those who have had a NDE.

1. Lack of words to express the experience (Ptolemy said it's impossible to visualize a higher dimension)

---

[1] Recollections of death p.152

2. A sense of timelessness (Einstein said time is an illusion)

3. An awareness of death in the conventional context *"We are confident, I say, and would prefer to be away from the body and at home with the Lord."* **2 Corinthians 5:8** (Separation from the body —- hovering over one's body)

4. A feeling of well being (euphoria, ecstasy)

5. Absence of pain: *"He will wipe every tear from their eyes. There will be no more death or mourning or crying or pain, for the old order of things has passed away."* **Revelation 21:4**

6. Being of a younger, healthier age: *"Who, by the power that enables him to bring everything under his control, will transform our lowly bodies so that they will be like his glorious body."* **Philippians 3:21**

7. Body looked like a dead worm (fourth dimensional long body): *"Do not be afraid, O worm Jacob, O little Israel, for I myself will help you."* **Isaiah 41:14**

8. Bright light that didn't hurt the eyes: *"About noon as I came near Damascus, suddenly a bright light from heaven flashed around me."* **Acts 22:6**

9. Reality of being alive greater than before the present state: "I have come that they may have life." ***John 10:10***

10. Perceptions of object more acute.

11. Light at the end of the tunnel (Wormhole?)

12. Perception of entering a location of ethereal beauty, beyond words. But as it is written, *"Eye hath not seen, nor ear heard, neither have entered into the heart of man, the things which God hath prepared for them that love him."* **1 Corinthians 2:9**

13. Religious views strengthened, but no increased desire to die.

The verses cited do not necessarily refer to a NDE, but are used to indicate the experiences are consistent with our general concept of heaven.

14. A consistent part of almost everyone's experience was entering or visualizing a place of bright light. This of course is a fundamental belief that when we enter the presence of God it will be associated with bright light. e.g.

"I will not rest, until the righteousness thereof go forth as brightness." **Isaiah 62:1** *"The court was full of the brightness of the LORD'S glory."* **Ezekiel 10:4** *"I saw a light from heaven, brighter than the sun, blazing around me and my companions."* **Acts 26:13**

Anecdotal accounts of near death experiences are not scientific evidence of the validity of an NDE. However, one must also recognize that conclusions by scientists are not evidence that NDE are not valid. In the context of my hyperdimensional theory, it is interesting that the anecdotal accounts are compatible with the paradigm of time-space we have been discussing.

In Chapter Two, (It's Time—To Understand) we constructed a concept of a person's hyperdimensional body. This body has a tangible linear time measurement beginning at conception and terminating at an event we call death. In other words, the time-space length of the body is measured in minutes, hours, days, months and years. This is not just a time measurement but a physical measurement as well.

This worm-like creature is motionless on the time plane and occupies a place designated between two dates on a calendar. (Birth date and date of death) In earlier chapters, we argued that past, present and future are only a stubbornly persistent illusion[2] created by viewing the landscape of reality through a narrow slit in the curtain of time. Therefore, our lives are not defined by the narrow slit in the time curtain but as a total entity from birth till death.

As individuals who are captives to the passage of time, we do not perceive the reality of a continuing physical existence. We consider our bodies to be real only in the immediate present. The past is gone and we are totally ignorant about what the future holds. Let's use an analogy that puts the concept of death in perspective.

You get on a train going to Florida from Boston with your mother, father, brother and two sisters. Your father has business in New York (code name 1967) and so he gets off

---

[2] Hyperspace,p.232

the train there. Your mother gets off in Baltimore (code 1978) to visit friends. Your two sisters decide to sightsee in Charleston, S.C.(code 1992) and you and your brother continue on to your destination in Florida (code 2020).

You have said goodbye to your father, mother and two sisters. Just because they are no longer on the train with you doesn't mean they're dead, even though the train is carrying you further and further away from them. The fact that you can't see them, talk to them, or make the train go backwards to where they are doesn't mean they're not still alive. It just means you have been separated from them by time and space. This is exactly what happens when a person's life terminates. They get off the "time-space" train and you continue on. I'm reasonably sure the person is still alive in the "NOW" of the past.

There are scriptures that support this: *"And after my skin has been destroyed, yet in my flesh I will see God; I myself will see him with my own eyes—I, and not another."* **Job 19:26-27**

When Christians die they are detached from their earthly connections and their hyperdimensional (spiritual) body passes through a wormhole into heaven. Near death experiences confirm this.

Christians who have a near death experience tell of going through a dark tunnel with a bright light at the end and a heavenly personage (Jesus) talking to them. Interestingly, in the studies mentioned above, this person to whom they were talking was seldom if ever seen.

My concept is that our hyperdimensional body, after entering this region of light, sleeps until judgment day. *""Our friend Lazarus has fallen asleep; but I am going there to wake him up."* **John 11:11** *"So then He told them plainly, Lazarus is dead."* **John 11:14** *"For when David had served God's purpose in his own generation, he fell asleep; he was buried with his fathers and his body decayed."* **Acts 13:36** *"Behold, I show you a mystery; We shall not all sleep, but we shall all be changed."* **1 Corinthians 15:51** *"We believe that Jesus died and rose again and so we believe*

*that God will bring with Jesus those who have fallen asleep
in him." 1 Thessalonians 4:14*

This is an interesting provision of the Lord, because if
we assume the long body theory is correct, the Christian
would be surrounded on the earthly time-space plane by the
wickedness of the unsaved existing during his life span. God
spares us from this association by putting our earthly bodies
into an ephemeral sleep. Even though our material body
sleeps our spiritual body is present with the Lord. *"We are
confident, I say, and willing rather to be absent from the
body, and to be present with the Lord." 2 Corinthians 5:8*
This is not true of the unsaved. I believe they experience a
universal "NOW" awareness of every sin of omission and
commission they have committed during their entire life and
they become acutely aware that for these sins they are facing
judgment and damnation. The worst realization will be that
they rejected the Salvation that would have blotted out those
sins.

For them there is no escape, no second chance to change
their lives. They've been frozen into their long body with
every evil thought, every despicable deed and every vile
desire they ever had. For the Christian, there is a different
picture.

Based on what the Bible tells us and within the construct
of hyperdimensional reality let me fabricate an allegory of
our walk into an unknown future.

Time is a blindfold over our eyes. We blindly stumble
along the path of life. Sometimes the road is smooth, and we
dance and sing as we take each step into the unknown.
Sometimes briers dig into our skin, and rocks cause us to
stumble and fall. For some the road is steep and rocky; for
others it may be all downhill; - - - a reckless pleasure ride
toward the brink of the abyss we call eternity. There is no re-
prieve, no slowing of the pace, sick or well, injured or
whole, time drags us forward to join the specter of death,
with no regard for who, or what we are. Relentlessly, we are
forced into the future.

Penetrating the sounds of laughter, the cursing of misfortune, the cries of pain, and the screams of terror rising from the crowd walking that treacherous road, there's a gentle, compassionate voice, saying, "Take my hand. When you fall, I'll help you up. I'll bandage your wounds. I'll carry you when you don't think you can take another step, and I'll lead you along the safest path available. When you come to the abyss, I'll not forsake you.?"

And so I take His hand and together we walk into a future I cannot see. But the strong, firm grip on my hand gives me confidence to take the next step. I don't know where the edge of the abyss is, which step will be my last, but I'm no longer afraid.

Finally, my companion says, "We've reached the end of the road and I'm going to take your blindfold off."

The blindfold drops from my eyes. I'm on the edge of a bottomless void, and now I can see clearly. A cross has fallen across the abyss forming a narrow bridge spanning the chasm. It leads to a land of green fields, sunshine and blue skies. But the cross is stained with blood. There are deep holes in the wood where spikes were driven. I look along the edge of the chasm and see thousands of people falling into the abyss. My companion is still holding my hand, and tears are pouring down His cheeks.

"I begged them to let me lead them to safety but they wouldn't listen," He explained. With that He lifts me in His arms and carries me safely to the other side of the abyss.

Time is a blindfold that God uses to protect us from the selfish, catastrophic behavior we would engage in if we could see the future. Only when we become Christians can we be trusted in an eternity where we are no longer a slave to time.

Chapter Fourteen
Windows To Heaven

The Bible tells us a great deal about heaven and ever-lasting life. In the thousands of sermons and Bible studies I've listened to over the past eighty years, I've never heard one that linked these ethereal concepts to the reality of established scientific theory. Many theologians think this can't be done, but they are wrong. The God who created this universe lives, moves and has His being in hyperdimensional reality. While God is not confined to such reality, He expresses Himself in it. The Bible tells us of substantive material in the "NOW" of the hereafter, such as thrones, cities, rivers, trees, roads, food, etc.

Although we will have new bodies they will be bodies of substance, with flesh and bone. Jesus said, *"Touch me and see; a ghost does not have flesh and bones, as you see I have...our body will be like His glorious body."* **Luke 24:38-39** Following his resurrection he was touched by human hands. **John 20:27** He ate food, wore clothes and carried on audible conversation, an act that requires physical anatomical structures. Heaven is a place of material substance.

Now for a big surprise, the Bible doesn't say we are going to spend our time in heaven. I think we will have access to heaven and be able to visit there, but the Bible teaches we will spend our time here on a new earth. Furthermore, God has prepared a city, the New Jerusalem, which will descend from heaven and become an earthly city.

This all sounds very mystical, but the reality of how it will happen is already being understood, in terms of modern science, in a remarkable way. First of all, we must understand when this happens "time" as we understand it will cease. This new heavenly civilization will exist on a five dimensional time-space plane with no past, present or future.

The Bible tells us that "time" will be understood in a divine framework, where a day is as a thousand years and a thousand years is as a day. In previous chapters, we have discovered that "time", as commonly thought of, is an illusion. There will not be an endless procession of days, months and years. Every possible legitimate activity past, present and future will be available to experience in the "NOW" of eternity.

A beautiful provision of this concept is that there will be no temptation to sin, because we can see what's ahead of us on the time-space plane; we will understand and appreciate the full consequences of every contemplated act to ourselves, to others and to God. There will be so many wonderful, creative things to do that the harmful, sinful options will hold no attraction for us.

Let me give you a personal glimpse of the kind of heaven I anticipate.

The night air was still and cool. The classic old world cathedral which dominated the town square thrust its spires and buttresses toward heaven etching a noble profile against the starlit sky. Only a few lights flickered in the windows of the dilapidated buildings surrounding the nearly deserted plaza. The adobe construction and the Spanish architecture made it seem like an ancient painting by a Castilian artist.

I stood on the balcony of my primitive hotel room hypnotized by the picturesque beauty that lay before me. Suddenly the night became alive with sound; silver notes from the bells in the cathedral carillon reverberated through the plaza. People appeared from nowhere and were drawn through the majestic arches of the cathedral as if by a giant magnet. It was time for me to go.

The Mexico City Symphony was to give a concert in the cathedral and I was anticipating a glorious evening of music. I hurried down to the square and joined the stream of people entering the place of worship. The wooden benches filled quickly and soon a hush fell over the audience. The conductor took the podium, raised his baton and the regal notes of Beethoven's *Overture to Fidelio* filled the air.

There was an immobilizing beauty about the setting. The town was in the major silver-producing region of Mexico, but in spite of its wealth there were no electric lights. The cathedral was lighted entirely by candles. Silver was everywhere; statues, crosses and icons glittered in the flickering light; shadows played hide and seek with the dazzling reflections from the polished precious metal and the majestic music from the orchestra lent an ethereal quality to the cavernous space of the nave above us. I sat transfixed by the sights and sounds of my surroundings. Could heaven be like this?

My scientific theories not only told me it would be similar, but that it would be infinitely better. My mind wandered to the amazing possibilities of what heaven would be like. The great Christian musicians of all time would gather together in one giant symphony orchestra. Sharing the stage would be the combined choirs of perfectly trained voices from ages past, ready to sing praises to our Lord and King.

In previous chapters, scientific evidence was presented showing that our resurrection bodies would have similar, but more perfect capabilities than our present ones. The Bible promises that we will be new creation. *"Therefore, if anyone is in Christ, he is a new creation; the old has gone, the new has come."* **2 Corinthians 5:17** When we become Christians our new bodies are already in the making. Jesus said we would have bodies like his glorious body. *"Who shall change our vile body, that it may be fashioned like unto his glorious body."* **Philippians 3:21**

There will be music and song, *"And they sing the song of Moses the servant of God, and the song of the Lamb, saying, Great and marvelous are thy works, Lord God Almighty; just and true are thy ways, thou King of saints."* **Revelation 15:3** But the interesting thing is that we can be doing different things at the same time, With five dimensional bodies in a timeless existence, we can have a three dimensional presence at two events simultaneously in different places and at different periods on the time-space plane and enjoy both them just as much as if they were seen in sequence.

It will be like at a movie or a video taken of your life from beginning to end, except that you will actually be present at every point in the movie, in your three dimensional appearance, at whatever time you choose, doing the thing that's happening in that part of the movie. At the same time, you may be doing something else in a different segment of your life somewhere else on the time-space plane.

The activities of a part of your long body of the past will not interfere with the activities carried out by another segment of your long body in the present, any more than what you did three years ago interferes with what you are doing today. The "NOW" of both segments are being carried out simultaneously in their three dimensional configuration without interference with each other. There is no break in the physical continuity of your body from then until now, but you perceive yourself in both instances in a three-dimensional form.

The difference is that instead of a movie you are experiencing two separate events at the same time in the "NOW" of different segments of your long time body; a "NOW" you can modify or completely change to suit your interest.

Dreams are wonderful vehicles to illustrate hyperdimensional concepts. In dreams, changing instantaneously from one time to another, or from one place to another, seems perfectly natural. The other night I had a weird dream that illustrates the above point.

I dreamt my family and I had gone to a concert in a strange city. On our way back to our hotel we got lost and had to stop and ask directions. We drove up to a roadside tavern and went in to ask the way to our hotel. My adult son asked the clerk behind the counter the correct way to go. The strange part of the dream was that in my dream I was holding the hand of a six-year-old child, and that child was the same person as the adult son who was asking directions. He was physically present with me in the tavern at two entirely different ages and sizes at the same time. In my dream, the situation didn't seem the least unusual, but when I awoke I had the eerie feeling I had temporarily escaped the restraints of this three dimensional world and had a hyperdimensional experience.

I've never had a dream before where the same person was present in the dream at different ages at the same time. One would obviously say such a thing is impossible. But is it?

Looking back on the previous material we've discussed, we assumed our long bodies would be resurrected. If this is true, I doubt if the fourth dimensional temporal length will be an encumbrance; we'll function and perceive ourselves and others in our three dimensional configuration, but as six dimensional beings we will be able move our state of awareness to whatever portion of our long body we prefer. We can be a three year old playing in the sand at the beach, or an elderly person on a cold day sitting in front of a blazing fire with a hot cup of tea and a friendly dog curled up at our feet.

The Bible gives us a hint that things will be like this. We are told we will be in the temple of God continually praising Him. In parables Jesus says we will also be governing cities, *Luke 19:17* acting as judges, *"Do you not know that we will judge angels? How much more the things of this life!?"* *1 Corinthians 6:3* eating, *"To him who overcomes, I will give some of the hidden manna."* *Revelation 2:17* drinking, *"That ye may eat and drink at my table in my kingdom."* *Luke 22:30* and doing an infinite number of other pleasurable, creative and constructive things.

Some of these activities will be going on simultaneously. I'm sure there are no contradictions in these assumptions. The hyperdimensional long body theory (which has a scientific basis) gives plausibility to the accuracy of all the statements that appear to be contradictory.

For me, this is the most exciting chapter in the book. I think very few people have a realistic view of heaven. I've heard numerous scenarios, and none of them depict the fantastic possibilities that can be achieved by blending accepted theories of science and Biblical descriptions of the hereafter.

The thrill of continually praising God for ten billion, billion years will be no different the last of those years than it was the first moment you began. (Because there is no passage of ten billion years; it's always "NOW". The first time thrill is always present. There will be no boredom from repetition and there will be appropriate movement within framework of the experience. It will not be the frozen landscape we are trapped in now. *"In the same way, we can see and understand only a little about God now, as if we were peering at his reflection in a poor mirror; but someday we are going to see him in his completeness, face to face.* ***Now all that I know is hazy and blurred, but then I will see everything clearly, just as clearly*** *as God sees into my heart right now."* ***1 Corinthians 13:12***

Every moment will be filled with the awe, the joy, and the reverence of the first moment you entered God's presence. Part of your long body is anchored there in an attitude of adoration, worship and praise. We will never leave, and never want to leave. Other parts of our long body will be carrying out tasks God has given us to do. Each repetition of every useful, beautiful and pleasurable event will be as thrilling as its first occurrence.

Remember "time" is not passing. "NOW" is everywhere; past present and future no longer exist. The western world looks at "time " as a rushing river; the Orientals look at time as a placid lake from which you can dip as much "time" as you need for whatever you are doing. The concept of 'time' being a lake is more consistent with my view of heaven.

In addition to wondering about our physical configuration and our concept of 'time' in heaven, there are other aspects of our after-life that are of much greater general interest, one of which is, "Will our departed pets be in heaven?"

This is a fascinating question. C. S. Lewis suggests it would be in the harmony with God's love to have our pets in heaven waiting for us. Of course, this is pure speculation, but Scripture teaches there are going to be animals in heaven, and they may even be able to talk to us. I'm not sure I want to hear what some of my pets might want to say to me. The precedent for this comes from two accounts in the Bible. The first is from **Genesis 3:1-3** *"Now the serpent was more crafty than any of the wild **animals** the LORD God had made. He said to the woman."* Did God really say, *"You must not eat from any tree in the garden?"* The serpent is referred to as an animal that talked and he is having a normal conversation with Eve.

The other reference is the episode with Balaam and the ass. *"Then the LORD opened the donkey's mouth, and she said to Balaam, "What have I done to you to make you beat me these three times? Balaam answered the donkey, "You have made a fool of me! If I had a sword in my hand, I would kill you right now."* **Numbers 22:28-29**

Other verses indicate there will be a variety of tame animals in heaven.

"The wolf also shall dwell with the lamb, and the leopard shall lie down with the kid; and the calf and the young lion and the fatling together; and a little child shall lead them. And the cow and the bear shall feed; their young ones shall lie down together: and the lion shall eat straw like the ox. And the sucking child shall play on the hole of the asp, and the weaned child shall put his hand on the cockatrice' den. They shall not hurt nor destroy in all my holy mountain: for the earth shall be full of the knowledge of the LORD, as the waters cover the sea." **Isaiah 11:5-9**

What about our sensual pleasures? We have talked about eating, drinking, singing and working in heaven, but there is still another question seldom addressed in the Christian community. In my passage through life, I've found that there is a great deal of unexpressed anxiety about whether we will have sexual feelings in our afterlife. This concern is real and it's important. It cuts across the concepts of every culture and religion, and it certainly must have crossed the mind of every Christian at one time or another.

Are we going to be sexually active in heaven?

I understand the Mormons believe they are going to raise families on their own planets somewhere in the far reaches of the universe.

Men in the Arabic countries think that if they give their lives in a suicide raid for their god Allah and their country, they will be given seventy-two beautiful virgins for their sexual pleasure. Ancient cultures such as the Greeks and Romans had Gods that were sexually active, and other cultures worshiped Gods and Goddesses of fertility. In Biblical times, God was continually opposing idolatrous sexual practices in heathen religions.

Let's look at this question from a logical point of view and come to some reasonable conclusion about this arcane subject. The Bible states there will be no marriage in heaven; we will be like the angels. *"At the resurrection people will neither marry nor be given in marriage; they will be like the angels in heaven."* **Matthew 22:30**

I think one of the reasons for this is that there will be no need for procreation. Jesus with His divine understanding of the conditions in heaven was aware of the problems that continued procreation would cause. Can you imagine the population growth during a billion years, with no attrition from accident or disease, and every baby having eternal life? The exponential growth of the population of heaven would be astronomical.

Would there be birth control? I don't think so. Secondly, I think this verse infers we will lose our individual sexual identity. When Jesus says we will be like the angels he does not say what the angels are like. He just says they don't marry, so we don't know what our sexual state will be like.

This is very disturbing to many individuals. They cherish their sexual identity and their sexual virility. They can't imagine supreme happiness in an eternity devoid of sex. Most Christians will tell you there will be no sexual relationships in heaven.

I think unequivocally we will not have the same biological sex drive for procreation that we have in this life, but don't despair there may be a better alternative. Sexual attraction as expressed in our everyday life, is primarily for the purpose of procreation. It's one of the strongest and most primitive drives of both animal and human behavior. God designed it that way to perpetuate the species.

But in the human species God introduced another element, that of sexual relationships purely for the pleasure associated with the manifestation of love. In its highest and purest form, the physical response to sexual intimacy is a byproduct of an intense desire for oneness with one's mate, and not just a need to satisfy a biological urge. In other words, sex without love and a passionate commitment to the needs, the welfare, and the pleasure of one's spouse is a distortion of the primary intent of sex for pleasure.

Now the question arises, as to whether it's possible to experience the exquisite sensations of physical and emotional pleasure associated with sex without the involvement of genital stimulation? We have separated sexual pleasure into physical desire, and emotional and spiritual commitment. This being true, my assumption is that it is not only possible, but also probable that we will have physiological and emotional capabilities to have physical, emotional and spiritual sensory experiences far beyond our most vivid imagination.

I'm proposing this because the Bible indicates heaven is going to be a place of perfect and complete fulfillment of our entire God-given desires. We know from Scripture that we will be given new physical bodies devoid of defects. As mentioned above, we will eat fantastic food and slake our thirst with heavenly beverages. If we eat exotic food and drink heavenly beverages for pleasure, as well as for nourishment and hydration, it seams reasonable to assume God is interested in our total ability to enjoy the other sensory pleasures He created our bodies to appreciate.

Certainly the ability to love with passion is one of God's most precious gifts. Is it not reasonable to assume He has also made provision for us to enjoy the pure intense sensory pleasure of love without the biological and physical involvement of the genital organs?

There is no room for lust in such fulfillment, because the relationship will be motivated by perfect love, not by a selfish biological urge. Since there is no need for procreation and no desire for selfish indulgence, we will be able to express our love for one another in exciting physical, emotional and spiritual ways, beyond anything we can humanly comprehend.

As a physician, I can tell you there is no other sensual experience that equals the combined physical, physiological and emotional response embodied in the intimate relationship between husband and wife when each one feels a love that's expressed by a total abandonment of oneself to the other.

When this sacred relationship is diluted or contaminated by any other motivation, it arouses terrible divine anger. It's like mixing rotten eggs in a delightful, delicate perfume. In my opinion, this relationship was so important to God He chose the custom of circumcision to emphasize the importance and sacredness of a sexual relationship.

Instead of circumcision why didn't He consider cutting off an ear lobe or tattooing a symbol on the hand or forehead? And what's so different in sexual misbehavior than the other sins of the flesh. It's the demeaning use of a precious sacrament designed to bind two lives together. From the sixth chapter of Genesis to the nineteenth chapter of Revelation, the Bible equates sex outside of the monogamous relationship of marriage between a man and a woman with sin.

Sex has been perverted to become the motivation of some of the most heinous acts of human behavior. Molestation of children and adults, torture, rape, murder, pornography and sadism have replaced the tender surrender of one's body and soul to the tender loving arms of a faithful mate.

In my twenty years of practicing psychiatry, I have seen sex used as an expression of anger, rage, sadism, selfish manipulation, bribery, immaturity, retaliation and other associated deviant behaviors. One can't imagine the magnitude of God's rage at humans who desecrate and destroy this very special and sacred gift.

Society is making a cataclysmic slide into a lust for physical pleasure. As society relaxes its sexual mores, it finds that the hedonistic freedom it is seeking is binding it more securely to a life of frustration and unhappiness. Yet it struggles even harder for greater liberties in sexual expression and sink even deeper into the quicksand of sin.

The exponential dominance of sex in entertainment, advertising, business, recreation, clothing, politics and health is frightening. The more explicit it gets more is desired. The drive is never satisfied. When the public gets what it asks for it finds it isn't enough. It's an insatiable lust driving our nation to destruction.

On the radio the other day, I heard a wonderful allegory that describes this situation perfectly.

A hunter wanted a bearskin coat, so he took his rifle and went out in the woods to find a bear. Soon, he came across a bear with a beautiful thick shiny coat. He raised his rifle and sighted it between the bear's eyes for a quick kill. He was about to pull the trigger when the bear said to him.

"Pardon me sir, but before you pull the trigger could we have a little talk?"

The amazed hunter, not being sure what to do with such a polite bear said, "Why certainly."

The bear said, "Sir, What do you want?"

The hunter said "I want a bearskin coat."

The bear said, "Well sir, I want a full stomach. It seems our desires are incompatible, but perhaps we can negotiate a settlement that will achieve the goals of each of us. Let's go back in the woods a little way and discuss this further."

The hunter agreed.

A short time later the bear came out alone.

The moral of the story is that the bear had a full stomach and the hunter had a bearskin coat.

Society is negotiating with a sexual predator for a bearskin coat and is going to end up being consumed.

The Song of Solomon makes no reference to God. I think this is because it's an implicit message from God to our very human nature establishing a prototype of what He intended our relationship should be with our spouse and lover. When one reads this book, one feels the warmth, the yearning, the ecstasy and the loving abandonment of giving oneself to another person on an emotional and spiritual level.

With sexuality referred to in the Scriptures so often, both in its supreme expression and its horrible degradation, one can't ignore the importance of God's purpose in creating sexual pleasure in humans and His disgust and anger at it's horrible desecration.

There are scriptures telling us we are going to enjoy other sensual pleasures, and although the manner in which we enjoy the physical consummation of a love relationship here on earth may be different in heaven, its manifestation will still be linked to utterly unselfish love, with an associated sensory experience beyond our wildest imagination.

Yes, our eternal home is real in physical and sensory ways that are seldom appreciated. We have a terrible time trying to separate the wonderful capabilities of sensual pleasure given to us by God, from mankind's catastrophic abuse of those capabilities. But how can we make sure we will ever reach this place of extraordinary existence. A true personal experience with a fantasy sequel will tell you how.

✦   ✦   ✦   ✦   ✦

The ancient box of pictures probably hadn't been opened for over fifty years. What memories did it grasp in its gnarled, withered hands? I picked up a portrait folder, blew the dust from the gray brown cover and opened it. There, with my brother and two sisters, I stood in serene splendor in my green velvet suit.

Memories cascaded over my mind; they were as clear as if it were yesterday. Again, I heard my mother call, as she came in the door, "Hi kids, I have wonderful news for you."

My mother was brimming over with excitement as she called our family together. "We're going to have the experience of a lifetime. We have been invited to a private reception for President Harding."

Though only six years old, I knew this was a big deal. We were not accustomed to circulating in such rarified segments of society. My father was the minister of a small church. He received no salary and we barely survived on free will offerings, plus an occasional bag of groceries from one of our parishioners. Families, whose children had outgrown their clothing, donated much of what we wore. God always supplied our needs and we were always warm and well fed, but our wardrobe was not suitable for a presidential reception.

The invitation had come from my Uncle Irwin, my mother's brother. He was the United States senator from Maryland, and a multi-millionaire. He lived in a palatial house on Mount Vernon Place in Baltimore, where the reception was to be held.

Naturally, he did not want to present his relatives to the president of the United States in mismatched, hand-me-down clothes and so he arranged to have us outfitted with the best clothes money could buy.

The big day was approaching and my mother and I went downtown to Baltimore's best department store. The clerk brought out a very expensive suit. I couldn't believe what was happening. The suit was green velvet, and was more beautiful than anything I'd ever seen. The short pants came to my knees and the jacket fit perfectly over a white shirt with a wide fluted collar. This was pulled together with a short white tie. Next, came black, knee length socks and shiny, black, high top leather shoes. When I looked in the mirror, I felt like a storybook prince.

The morning of the reception I awoke bursting with excitement. The gas water heater had been on for over an hour. My brother and sisters had already taken their baths. My mother hustled me into the tub and scrubbed me as I had never been scrubbed before. Then, I dressed in my new clothes. When I looked in the mirror, I looked like an English lord.

About 10:30 A.M., Andrus, my uncle's chauffeur, drove to our front door in a shiny black Packard Town Car. There was a glass partition between the front seat and the back and there was a phone in the back so you could talk to the driver. My father sat in the front seat with the chauffeur and my mother, with her four children, sat in the back. In the back there were two jump seats that folded down. I got to sit on one of them. The drive to my uncle's house took only fifteen minutes. When we arrived many of the guests were already there. I saw the long row of black limousines parked at the curb and members of the Secret Service inconspicuously inspecting every new arrival.

My Aunt Evalyn was the hostess. (We called her Aunt Beauty) She greeted us at the door and ushered us into a small anti-room.

She said, "Now remember when you go through the reception line take the person's hand and say, 'I'm very pleased to meet you,' and go on to the next person."

The reception was in a large ballroom just to the left of the entrance hall. The light from the crystal chandeliers reflected their elegance in the gilt framed mirrors. Vases of fresh flowers were tastefully arranged around the room.

The receiving line was long, consisting of senators and other dignitaries. Among the women present were Grace Coolidge, wife of Vice President Calvin Coolidge, and Tallulah Bankhead, the famous actress.

I started down the line and very obediently and properly took the first person's hand, gave it a single shake and said, "I'm very pleased to meet you." Then, I came to the President.

My aunt put her hand on my shoulder and said, "President Harding, I would like to introduce my nephew, William Nesbitt, Jr."

After saying the same thing fifteen times to the preceding fifteen people, I thought it was time for a change. I looked up at the President, took a deep breath and said, "Hello." The receiving line burst into laughter. The President smiled, took my hand and said, "It's a pleasure to meet you, young man."

It was a memorable experience, but as the warmth of those memories floated through my mind the scene faded and in its place another vision materialized.

I'm preparing for another reception, one much more impressive than the one for the president of the United States. I'm invited to a royal reception of unparalleled magnificence, but one in which the circumstances are much the same as the situation I have just described.

I'm poor, my clothes are ragged and my shoes worn through. I have tried to wash myself, but there's dirt under my nails and behind my ears. My hair is matted and I need to brush my teeth.

What am I going to do? I can't go to this wonderful event looking like this. In the midst of my despair, there was a knock on the door. It was Jesus; He looked at me and winced.

"You're not ready, are you?

I began to cry. "I've tried, but I can't do it by myself."

"I know you can't. That's why I'm here. I have come to get you ready. When you see our Father, He will expect you to be sparkling clean and properly clothed. He's expecting us, so we must hurry and get ready."

I've never had such a scrubbing before. He literally sweat great drops of blood to get me clean. He cleaned away hidden dirt that I didn't even know was there. The dirt behind my ears and under my nails that I couldn't get rid of disappeared under His meticulous cleansing. My hair was washed, trimmed and combed. Now it was time to get dressed, "But what am I going to wear?" I asked.

He went over to the table and opened a suit box that he had brought. He took out the most beautiful clothes I've ever seen."

I made sure these would fit you perfectly," He said. Then He clothed me in the garments of salvation and arrayed me in the robe of His righteousness.[1] The clothes were made of white linen, without spot or wrinkle, and He gave me the

---

[1] Isaiah 61:10

gospel of peace to wear on my feet. Never in my life had I looked so good.

Now it was time to go.

When we arrived at the reception Jesus said, "I must leave you now and take my place in the receiving line. Just get in that line over there, tell the people how glad you are to be here, and how happy you are to meet them. I will see you soon."

There were thousands in the receiving line, relatives and friends, patriarchs, apostles, saints, evangelists, theologians, martyrs, prophets and other mighty warriors of God that I had never heard of before. I didn't know how long it was taking me to progress through the line. I forgot that time had vanished and I was living in an eternal present. Fatigue was non-existent, only the excitement of the present filled my mind.

Finally, I reached the front of the line. There was Jesus, standing at the right hand of God. Trembling, I stepped forward and Jesus said, 'This is Bill Nesbitt, a very precious member of our family.

I was transfixed. The glory surrounding the throne was like ten thousand suns. Spread out at God's feet a new heaven and the new earth vibrated with exuberant life. The universe was no longer motionless and shackled by sin. Behind the throne was the deep blue curtain of outer space. Stars and galaxies showered their brilliance in a backdrop of unprecedented magnificence. It was beauty, power and love beyond my ability to perceive. There was no barrier of aloofness, no aura of intimidation. I was a polished mirror reflecting the love of the Creator in all of its redemptive per-fection.

I fell at His feet with trembling lips and said, "Abba Father, thank you for loving me so much that you gave the life of your only begotten son, Jesus, so I could be here.

God smiled, reached down and took my hand, helping me to my feet. He said, " Bill, I love you so much, way beyond your comprehension. I'm so glad you're here. But you know, there are lots of my children named Bill, and when I call you I want you to know it is you I am calling, so I am giving you a new name. One different from everyone else. Then He said, "Come, it's time to get something to eat, I have a special treat for you."

He handed me a white stone and on that stone was engraved a name that only God and I would know, and it would be mine for all eternity.

"To him who overcomes, I will give some of the hidden manna. I will also give him a white stone with a new name written on it, known only to him who receives it." **Revelation 2:16**

✦   ✦   ✦   ✦   ✦

Dear reader are you going to be there with me to share the fantastic life of beauty, joy, and love God has prepared for us? Are you washed in the blood of the Lamb, clothed in the garments of salvation, and arrayed in the robe of His righteousness? God loves you more than you can possibly imagine. If you're not ready for this magnificent experience confess your sins, (All have sinned and come short of the glory of God) forgive those who have sinned against you, believe in the redemptive act of Jesus Christ and share with others the wonderful gift of salvation you have just received. God is expecting you. Don't disappoint Him.

Bibliography

Books and Other Reference Material

Direct quotes are referred to in footnotes. Materials listed in this section indicate the scope of background reading and other applicable reference material. Information from titles noted may or may not be included in the text of the manuscript, but it is included because of its impact on the thinking of the author. In the opinion of the author the most informative, lucid and complete information on Hyperdimensional Theory is the book *Hyperspace* by **Michio Kaku**

Non-fiction

Barbour, Julian, *The End of Time*, Oxford Press, 1999

Behe, Michael J., *Darwin's Black Box*, Touchstone Books, Simon and Schuster, New York, 1996

Bentley, Bill E.., *Angels are Real*, Bill Bentley Ministries, Lenoir, N.C., 1997

Cairns, A.G. – Smith, *Evolving the Mind,* Cambridge University Press, 1996

Cullmann, Oscar, *Christ and Time ,*S C M Press LTD,1962

Davies, Paul, *God and The New Physics*, Touchstone, Simon and Schuster, 1983

Dembski, William, *Mere Creation*, InterVarsity Press, Downers Grove, IL, 1998

Graham, Billy, *Angels*, Word Books, Waco TX, 1986

Granville, William Anthony, *The Fourth Dimension And The Bible*, The Gorham Press, Boston, MA 1922

Hawking, Stephen, *A Brief History of Time*, Bantam Books, New York, 1988 *Black Holes and Baby Universes*, Bantam Books, New York 1993

Hearn, Walter R., *Being A Christian In Science*, Intervarsity press, Downers Grove, IL, 1997

Hunter, Charles and Frances, *Angels On Assignment*, Hunter Books, Kingwood, TX, 1979

Johnson, Phillip, E., *Defeating Darwinism*, InterVarsity Press, Downers Grove, IL, 1997

Kaku, Michio, *Hyperspace*, Anchor Books, Doubleday, 1994

Kubler-Ross, Elisabeth, *On Death and Dying*, Macmillan Publishing Co., 1969

Lewis, C.S., *Mere Christianity*, Touchstone Books, Simon and Schuster, New York, NY, 1996

Monsma, John Clover (Edited By), *The Evidences of God*, G.P. Putman and Sons, New York, NY, 1958

Norris, Richard A., Jr. ,*The Christological Controversy*, Fortress Press, Philadelphia, PA, 1980

Ostrander, Shiela, and Schroeder, Lynn, *Psychic Discoveries Behind The Iron Curtain*, Prentice Hall, 1970

Ouspensky, P.D., *Tertium Organum*, Vintage Books, Random House, New York, NY, 1970

Padmanabhan, T., *After The First Three Minutes*, Cambridge University Press, New York, NY, 1994

Polkinghorn, John, *Quarks, Chaos, & Christianity.*, Crossroad Books, New York, NY, 1994

Rausch, William G. *The Trinitarian Controversy*, Fortress Press, Philadelphia, PA, 1980

Ross, Hugh, *The Fingerprint of God*, Promise Publishing Co., Orange, CA *Creator and The Cosmos*, Nav Press, Colorado Springs, CO, 1955 *The Genesis Question*, Nav Press, Colorado Springs, CO, 1998 *Beyond The Cosmos*, Nav Press, Colorado Springs, CO, 1996 Creation and Time, Nav Press, Colorado Springs, CO, 1994

Schroeder,, Gerald L., *The Science of God*, Broadway Books, New York, NY, 1997

Smoot, George, and Davidson, Keay, *Wrinkles In Time* , Avon Books, New York, NY, 1993

Targ, Russell and Harary, Kieth, *The Mind Race,* Villard Books, New York, NY, 1984

Tipler, Frank J. *The Physics of Immortality*, Doubleday, New York, NY, 1994

Warner, Rex, The *Confessions of St.Augustine, A Contemporary Translation*, A Mentor Book, (Signet) 1963

Waugh, Alexander, *Time*, Carroll and Graf Publishers, New York, 2000

Williams, Cora L. *Creative Involution*, California Press, San Francisco, CA, 1916

White, Michael, and Gribbin, John, *Stephen Hawking*, Penguin Books, New York, NY, 1992

Wolf, Fred, *Parallel Universes,* Touchstone , Simon and Schuster, New York, NY,1988

Youngblood, Ronald, *The Genesis Debate*, Thomas Nelson Publishers, Nashville, TN, 1986

Fiction

Crichton, Michael, *Timeline,* Ballantine Books, New York, NY, 1999

Schofield, A.T., *Another World*, George Allen & Unwin Ltd., Ruskin House, London, 1885

Significant Magazine Articles

Arkani-Hamed, Dimopoulos and Dvali, *The Universes Unseen Dimensions*, Scientific American, August 2000

A Special Report, *Brave New Cosmos*, Scientific American, January 2001

Bliwise, Robert J., *Contemplating Cosmic Convergence*, Duke Magazine, July-August 2000

Folger, Tim, *From Here To Eternity*, Discover Magazine, December 2000

Gould, Stephen Jay, *The Pre-Adamite Man in a Nutshell,* Discover Magazine, November 1999

Overbye, Dennis, *Before the Big Bang, There was...What ?,* Science Times, The New York Times, May 12, 2001

Rause, Vince, *Searching for the Divine*, Readers Digest, December 2001

Samples, Kenneth, *Thinking About the Trinity*, Facts For Faith, Reasons To Believe, Quarter 3, 2000

Weinberg, Steven, *Is the Universe Designed*, The New York Review of Books, October 21, 1999

Audio Tapes from the Teaching Company, Chantilly, Virginia

Markos, Louis, *The Life and Writings of C.S. Lewis*, Course 297

Robinson, Donald, *The Great Ideas of Philosophy*, Course 494

Sapolsky, Robert, *Biology and Human Behavior*, Course 179

Wolfson, Richard, *Einstein's Relativity and the Quantum Revolution*, Course 152

Audio Tapes From Other Sources

Christian Doctors Digest, Years 1999, 2000 & 2001

Message of the Month, *Reasons To Believe*, Years 2000 & 2001

In addition to the above references dozens of magazine articles, newspaper articles, science fiction books, movies, lectures and sermons have contributed to the general body of information of this work, and demonstrated the high degree of public interest in Time, Higher Dimensions and Metaphysics.

Glossary of Terms

Abstract thinking: Thinking about something that can't be pictured as a reality. Theoretical.

A-priori assumption: an assumption in advance that such evidence exists.

Astro-physics: A study of the physical science of the stars.

A timeless entity: Something that has no boundaries in time and space.

Ephemeral sleep: a transitory or temporary sleep.

Ethereal concept: A heavenly point of view.

Eternal reality: The perception we will have of things in the life hereafter.

4th, 5th, 6th, 7th, etc dimensions: The existence of non-Euclidian measurements beyond the normal three dimensions with which we are all familiar.

Gravitational (G) Forces: One of the three primary forces in the universe. (The one that attracts object to one another on the bases of their weight.)

Higher dimensions: Dimensions in addition to length, breadth and height.

Hyperdimensional reality: The assumption that there is substantive existence of things in higher dimensions outside the perception of our five senses.

Hyperspace: Time-space beyond our visible universe.

Holistic reality: An appreciation of the entire picture, rather than just an understanding of the individual parts.

Inter-dimensional travel: Travel between this universe and other universes in higher dimensions.

Linear time-space life (span): The length of ones fourth dimensional body on the five dimensional time-space plane of this universe.

Long body theory: Our bodies are a single physical unit from birth to death.

Metaphysical reality: The assumption that there is physical substance in some supernatural events.

Morality as being relative: Morality being judged by comparative standards rather than by the Bible.

NDE (Near death experiences): The stories of people who were declared clinically dead and then were resuscitated.

Parallel universes, (Mirror Universes): Material universes, similar to our universe, in other dimensions.

Parapsychology: The psychology of the metaphysical.

Parochial theory of time: The common understanding that time is an unchangeable entity.

Predeterminist: That events in the future already exist and are unchangeable.

Seven heavens: Seven parallel universes

Spiritual reality: That many spiritual events have a substantive quality as well as a theological one.

Static Universe: One in which nothing moves.

Subatomic particles: Particles of matter that are smaller than an atom.

Supernatural phenomena: Events that are not attributed to natural causes.

Supernatural reality: Substantive existence of spiritual things.

Temporal dimensions: Measurement of things in time as well as space.

The eternal "NOW": That everything that ever existed, that presently exist, and that ever will exist already exists as the present in the eyes of God.

Theoretical physics: The study of physics in areas that can not be physically demonstrated, but seem logically correct.

The theory of higher dimensions: The expansion of our three dimensional universe to include the possibility of additional dimensions, and other universes.

Time plane: Our universe is a flat time plane extending from its first appearance to its final dissolution.

Time-space plane theory: That everything that ever existed or ever will exist is motionless and already in place on the time-space plane of our universe.

Time warp: The opening of a wormhole between parallel universes.

Transpermia: A theory which proposes that an intelligent source somewhere in the far reaches of the universe seeded the earth with living organisms.

True lies: Lies with enough elements of truth to be considered valid, but the ultimate meaning is an outright lie.

Vertical dimension of time: The concept that time-space has three dimensions similar to the three physical dimensions with which we are familiar.

Wormholes: Portals of communication and travel between parallel universes.